F. Scott Fitzgerald

ANDREW HOOK

Bradley Professor of English Literature
University of Glasgow

Edward Arnold
A division of Hodder & Stoughton
LONDON NEW YORK MELBOURNE AUCKLAND

©1992 Andrew Hook

First published in Great Britain 1992

Distributed in the USA by Routledge, Chapman and Hall, Inc.
29 West 35th Street, New York, NY 10001

British Library Cataloguing in Publication Data

Hook, Andrew
    F. Scott Fitzgerald. – (Modern Fiction
    Series)
    I. Title II. Series
    813.52

    ISBN 0–340–54018–4

Typeset in 10/12pt Linotron Sabon by
'Anneset' Weston-super-Mare, Avon
Printed and bound in Great Britain for Edward Arnold,
the educational, academic and medical publishing division of
Hodder and Stoughton Limited, 41 Bedford Square, London
WC1B 3DQ by Biddles Ltd, Guildford & King's Lynn

General Editor: Robin Gilmour

Contents

General Editor's Preface   vi

Preface   vii

A Note on Editions   ix

1 Fitzgerald and the American Dream   1

2 *This Side of Paradise*   14

3 *The Beautiful and Damned*   30

4 *The Great Gatsby*   44

5 *Tender is the Night*   60

6 *The Last Tycoon*   76

Conclusion   86

Select Bibliography   89

Chronological Table   93

Index   95

General Editor's Preface

Fiction constitutes the largest single category of books published each year, and the discussion of fiction is at the heart of the present revolution in literary theory, yet the reader looking for substantial guidance to some of the most interesting prose writers of the twentieth century – especially those who have written in the past 30 or 40 years – is often poorly served. Specialist studies abound, but up-to-date maps of the field are harder to come by. *Modern Fiction* has been designed to supply that lack. It is a new series of authoritative introductory studies of the chief writers and movements in the history of twentieth-century fiction in English. Each volume has been written by an expert in the field and offers a fresh and accessible reading of the writer's work in the light of the best recent scholarship and criticism. Biographical information is provided, consideration of the writer's relationship to the world of their times, and detailed readings of selected texts. The series includes short-story writers as well as novelists, contemporaries as well as the classic moderns and their successors, Commonwealth writers as well as British and American; and there are volumes on themes and groups as well as on individual figures. At a time when twentieth-century fiction is increasingly studied and talked about, *Modern Fiction* provides short, helpful, stimulating introductions designed to encourage fresh thought and further enquiry.

Robin Gilmour

Preface

Scott Fitzgerald is one of the most popular of modern American writers. His fame and reputation are reflected in different ways: on the one hand our film and television screens offer us versions of his work, with big-name stars, with some regularity; on the other, the literature curricula of our schools, colleges, and universities feature at least some of his novels and stories even more frequently. At the same time, scholars and critics have found a great deal to say about Fitzgerald, his life and his work, with the result that it would be hard to argue that there is any shortage of widely available material concerning him. How then does one justify adding yet another item to an already overcrowded field?

There are two answers. The great bulk of existing secondary material on Fitzgerald focuses more or less exclusively on no more than two of his texts: *The Great Gatsby* above all, and, to a rather lesser extent, *Tender is the Night*. The overwhelming majority of essays and articles, and guides, concern themselves with one or other of these. This short study is different in so far as it attempts to consider Fitzgerald's work as a whole – though I am conscious that the short stories merit fuller treatment than they receive here – looking at each of Fitzgerald's novels in turn and paying as much attention to the early work as to the later. Each novel is considered in its own right, within the overall context of Fitzgerald's literary career, but I also try to show that a particular pattern of concerns recurs throughout Fitzgerald's writing life. What these concerns are relates to the ambiguous roles of man and writer: Fitzgerald discovered that the kind of man he was, and the kind of writer he needed to be, were difficult to reconcile. The recognition and exploration of this problem then becomes a unifying subtext in a great deal of his writing.

The second reason for writing this brief study is the existence of the series to which it belongs. A series called *Modern Fiction* could hardly afford to ignore Fitzgerald. The generation of American writers to which he belonged, so precociously talented, made a crucial contribution to the development of modern literary culture in English. The influence of these writers is still with us, their voices still speak to us, and no voice, not even that of Hemingway or Faulkner, speaks more clearly than Fitzgerald's.

How to write about Fitzgerald's voice today, however, is no easy matter. Much current literary theory encourages us to think in terms of the death of the author and the duplicitous life of the text. But in the case of Fitzgerald to attempt to separate the work from the man producing it is neither easy nor necessarily desirable. Even more than is true of most authors, Fitzgerald's life and art run in and out and through each other. Their inter-penetration is so complete that to try to deconstruct them would be artificial, unhelpful, and simply creating an unnecessary barrier to understanding. My own inclination as a literary scholar has always been towards an historical, contextual approach to the individual work of art. But over and over again I discover that in Fitzgerald's case, the context that really matters is his own life. Hence the critical approach which informs this short study of Fitzgerald might in practice be best described as a psycho-biographical one.

For giving me an opportunity to pursue my commitment to Fitzgerald – a commitment which predates even my own days at Princeton – I should like to extend my thanks to Robin Gilmour, General Editor of this series I am happy too to acknowledge the value of his editorial comments on my text. Finally I wish to express my gratitude to Ingrid Swanson, a meticulous and invaluable secretary who has done so much to make the production of this book possible.

Andrew Hook
Glasgow, 1991

Acknowledgement

The American Dream from the musical Miss Saigon by Alain Boublil and Claude-Michel Schonberg. Lyrics by Richard Maltby Jr. and Alain Boublil. Music by Claude-Michel Schonberg.

A Note on Editions

Throughout this study I have cited Penguin editions of Fitzgerald's works on the grounds that these are far and away the most readily available and the most likely to be in the possession of readers. However, readers should note that, particularly in the case of the most popular titles, constantly reprinted and reissued, minor variations in pagination do occur. *Tender is the Night* presents a special problem. Over the years Penguin Books have published different versions of this novel: both the original and the revised which alters the arrangement of the material. My references are to the most recent Penguin edition of the original version in larger format.

For Marcella

Heavens

Dear Scott Fitzgerald and Zelda in paradise
Oh heavens,
I hope the flames stopped dancing
Quickly Zee.
I see Scott on the road madly driving
To the asylum in his fame
Where hope fell over the cliff.
I hope that Switzerland road
Is covered with small and pale
Strong flowers like her hair
Before the fall, coloured champagne.

M.S.E.

1

Fitzgerald and the American Dream

I

The publication of his first novel *This Side of Paradise* in 1920 made Scott Fitzgerald famous and wealthy at the age of twenty-three. When he died in Hollywood in December, 1940, aged forty-four, he was struggling financially, and his fame and reputation as a writer had almost totally evaporated. In a letter to his wife Zelda, written in March, 1940, he described himself as 'a forgotten man,' and according to his friend and fellow-novelist John O'Hara, at the end of his life he was 'a prematurely old little man haunting bookstores unrecognized.'[1] His last royalty statement from Scribners, dated 1 August 1940, listed sales of forty copies of his books earning a royalty of thirteen dollars and thirteen cents. Yet half a century on, the wheel has once again come full circle, and Scott Fitzgerald is established as a classic American writer of the twentieth century. Every book and every story remains in print; his work has been translated into at least thirty-five languages; *The Great Gatsby* sells three hundred thousand copies a year in the USA alone; and of course the production of critical and biographical studies – like this one – is never ending.

The swings and roundabouts of literary reputations are a familiar story. But the case of Fitzgerald is an extreme one. What happened during his own life time is reasonably easy to understand. Even if nothing quite compared in his own mind with the first astonishing success of *This Side of Paradise*, the achievement of *The Great Gatsby*

[1]Quoted by Matthew J. Bruccoli, *Some Sort of Epic Grandeur: The Life of F. Scott Fitzgerald* (London, Sydney, Auckland, Toronto, 1981), p. 489.

(1925) confirmed Fitzgerald's reputation as a leader of a new postwar generation of American writers. But as the 20s faded into the 30s, and the success of *Gatsby* was not followed up, so Fitzgerald's standing began to slip. *Tender is the Night* finally appeared in 1934, but that novel was at best a partial success. Throughout the rest of the 30s the slide continued, and at his death in 1940 *The Last Tycoon* was only a fragment of an unpublished novel. Fitzgerald seemed destined to be remembered as at best a novelist who had failed to fulfil his early promise.

So what happened? How did the failure of 1940 become the literary classic of today? This transformation is less easy to explain, and no doubt many different kinds of factor are involved. At the heart of the matter one would like to think is Fitzgerald's basic quality as a writer: the ultimate fineness of his handling of language, what his friend John Dos Passos once called his development of 'an elegant and complicated piece of machinery,' a tool for writing, that was second to none.[2] That Fitzgerald's writing was second to none was exactly John O'Hara's view as he put it to John Steinbeck: 'Fitzgerald was a better just plain writer than all of us put together. Just words writing.'[3] But can one believe that this in itself was enough? Does quality in the end always tell? One fears probably not.

The most common explanation of the Fitzgerald renaissance sees it as occurring in the 1950s and relates it to the distinctive characteristics of American society and culture in that decade. What Robert Lowell described as 'the tranquillized *Fifties*' is generally regarded as a period of cold war conservatism and restraint. Thus the argument is that older American readers found a kind of nostalgic attraction in Fitzgerald's portrait of a very different Jazz Age America while, perhaps more importantly, younger readers responded enthusiastically to his creation of a world of freedom and liberation and the questioning of traditional values. In this sense the Fitzgerald revival seems almost to herald the cultural revolution of the 1960s. This account may well contain part of the truth – but it certainly needs to be qualified. Matthew J. Bruccoli, a leading Fitzgerald scholar, has argued cogently that the Fitzgerald revival was triggered by a *Gatsby* revival – and that the *Gatsby* revival occurred in the 1940s in the years immediately after Fitzgerald's death. Bruccoli tells us that between 1941 and 1949 there were seventeen new editions or reprints of *The*

[2] For the letter by Dos Passos in which the phrase occurs see p. 72 below.
[3] See Bruccoli, *Some Sort of Epic Grandeur*, p. 478.

Great Gatsby.[4] Thus it was reader demand as early as the 1940s that really signalled the revival of Fitzgerald's literary fortunes. This in turn led to the critical reappraisals, the burgeoning academic interest, and the widespread, general enthusiasm of the 1950s and the succeeding decades.

Of course, from the beginning, there were those like Malcolm Cowley who doubted whether the Fitzgerald vogue was sustainable, whether in fact Fitzgerald would prove to have the staying power of a major artist. (Given the conventional critical view – which I shall discuss in the next chapter – that Fitzgerald's literary successes were few in number, this view is perfectly understandable.) Nevertheless the doubters have been proved wrong. Fitzgerald's restored literary prestige shows no signs of declining: his classic status is unchallenged. My own explanation of the continuing and universal interest in Fitzgerald and his work will strike many readers as surprising. It is meant in no way to disparage Fitzgerald's quality purely as a writer – many people like to read Fitzgerald simply because he writes so well. But the Fitzgerald phenomenon, as it were, seems to require a more wide-ranging social and cultural explanation and what this is, in my view, involves centrally the notion of the American Dream. Fitzgerald's reputation as a major American author has been developed and sustained by the ever-increasing popularity of the concept of the American Dream. Only when the American Dream began to pass into the general consciousness of what people everywhere knew – or thought they knew – about America could the former chronicler of the Jazz Age be canonized as the poet of America and its lost hopes. Fitzgerald's reputation has been borne up and swept along by the notion of the American Dream.

Since the end of the Second World War the United States of America has been the most powerful country in the world. American power has included cultural power and in the definition of that power no term rivals the eminence that has been accorded to the American Dream. Everywhere and in every context the phrase occurs again and again; writing or talking about America means invoking the American Dream; journalists and television commentators would time and again be lost for words without it. Commentators and critics concerned with every aspect of America's cultural life turn to the concept with a predictable inevitability. All American literature – like all of American life – it often seems, is about the American Dream. But if this is true

---

[4]See Matthew J. Bruccoli, ed., *New Essays on The Great Gatsby* (Cambridge, London, New York, New Rochelle, Melbourne, Sydney, 1985), p. 5.

of American authors in general, of whom is it more true than F. Scott Fitzgerald? Fitzgerald has been identified with the American Dream. He above all is its poet and celebrant. As the postwar world became increasingly fascinated by American culture and its nature, and as in consequence the currency of the American Dream was diffused still more widely, perhaps it was inevitable that Fitzgerald's reputation as a writer would begin to rise. He had written about the American Dream – as every student required to write about *The Great Gatsby* now knows. It was his subject, his matter above all – and it was a subject that had come to fascinate readers everywhere.

But is it true? Did Fitzgerald write about the American Dream? And if he did, what did he understand by it? There are some difficulties. To start with, the term the American Dream seems not to have had any general currency in the 1920s – and even less in any earlier period. The first identifiable use of the phrase in the form that has become so familiar occurs in James Truslow Adams's book, *The Epic of America*, published in 1931. In the Preface to his book, Adams speaks of 'that American dream of a better, richer, and happier life for all our citizens of every rank which is the greatest contribution we have as yet made to the thought and welfare of the world.' In his Epilogue, Adams returns to what he calls America's 'distinctive and unique gift to mankind' – 'the *American dream*, that dream of a land in which life should be better and richer and fuller for every man, with opportunity for each according to his ability or achievement.' Notice how the word 'dream' remains uncapitalized: Adams does not offer the American Dream as an established, existing, universally recognized concept. Nevertheless, he is explicit in 1931 about what the American Dream is, in a way that Fitzgerald never was. Yet by the end of the 1930s, Fitzgerald could write directly of the American Dream. His notes for his unfinished last novel *The Last Tycoon* include the following comment on the history of America: 'I look out at it – and I think it is the most beautiful history in the world. It is the history of me and my people. . . . It is the history of all aspiration – not just the American dream but the human dream and if I came at the end of it that too is a place in the line of the pioneers.' So perhaps Fitzgerald did know in 1925 that *The Great Gatsby* was about the American Dream – even if the phrase itself remains the 'fragment of lost words' that Nick Carraway almost remembers as he listens to Gatsby's appallingly sentimental account of Daisy Buchanan at the end of Chapter Six.

Adams's statements in *The Epic of America*, and Fitzgerald's comment on American history, function in ways that go beyond the establishing of historical parameters for the use of the phrase the American Dream. They are timely reminders of the dimensions of meaning that the phrase itself encapsulates. This is important because the growing popularity of the phrase – the almost absurdly predictable regularity with which journalists and others deploy it – has gone hand in hand with an increasing vulgarization of its meaning:

> What's that I smell in the air?
> The American Dream
> Sweet as a new millionaire
> The American Dream
> Pre-packed ready-to-wear
> The American Dream
>
> . . .
>
> Busboys can buy the hotel
> The American Dream
> Wall Street is ready to sell
> The American Dream
> Come make a life from thin air
> The American Dream
> Come and get more than your share
> The American Dream.

What these lyrics sung by the engineer in the musical *Miss Saigon* do is reflect what the American Dream has come to mean at a popular level. The American Dream is the Success Story; the American Dream is the climbing of the ladder from rags to riches; the American Dream is from the log cabin to the White House; the American Dream is to go West, young man – and become a millionaire. In all these definitions the American Dream is conceived of in terms of success – and of material success in particular: getting rich quick is what it is all about. Yet this can hardly be what Fitzgerald had in mind when he described American history as beautiful, the history of all aspiration, of the human dream itself. And James Truslow Adams was quite explicit that the American Dream was not a dream 'of merely material plenty:' 'it has been,' he writes, 'much more than that.' Of course given the abject material circumstances that the vast majority of people in most countries of the world had been expected over long centuries, to accept as normal, it is not surprising that the dream of material well-being should have been part of the promise of America from the start. But the American Dream in its true sense has never been limited to material success alone.

If the lyrics from *Miss Saigon* represent a vulgarization and trivialization of the American Dream, what is the phrase's true meaning? The American Dream encompasses the myth of America: a myth defined and epitomized by another familiar phrase – the New World. In its origins, America was conceived of as quite literally a **new** world, offering humanity a new beginning, a second chance. The contrast of course was with Europe – the Old World – characterized by tyranny, corruption, and social divisions. Innocent of these, the New World was a kind of virgin land, pure and unfallen. Notions of this kind had surrounded the idea of America from the earliest days of its discovery by European explorers. But they were given an enormous boost by the political events of the later eighteenth century. The conclusion of the American Revolution, and the establishment of the new American republic, seemed to people on both sides of the Atlantic like the realization of a dream. The shackle of Europe, the burden of the European past, with its associated evils of social, political, and religious tyranny and corruption, had been thrown off. For all people of liberal persuasion, for all those dissatisfied with the status quo upheld by the ancien régimes of Europe, for all believers in democracy and the rights of man, America had apparently taken an enormous stride towards the realization of the dream of social equality and individual freedom.

In the work of the French writer, Hector St John de Crèvecoeur, we can find one of the earliest and most popular disseminations of this visionary, New World, America. In *Letters from an American Farmer*, published in London in 1782, Crèvecoeur contrasts Europe and America by associating Europe with history and the past, America with the future, and begins to set out the constituents of what will become the American Dream:

> Here [in America] we have had no war to desolate our fields; our religion does not oppress the cultivators: we are strangers to those feudal institutions which have enslaved so many. Here nature opens her broad lap to receive the perpetual accession of newcomers, and to supply them with food.

Whereas in Italy the traveller is surrounded by scenes of ruin and decay, 'Here he might contemplate the very beginnings and outlines of human society. . . .' Whereas in Europe 'misguided religion, tyranny, and absurd laws everywhere depress and afflict mankind': 'Here we have in some measure regained the ancient dignity of our species. . . .' As a result, humanity itself has been transformed: the American 'is a new man, who acts upon new principles; he must therefore entertain new ideas, and form new opinions.' And America itself is indeed the promised land, offering an unequivocal welcome to the European immigrant:

> Welcome to my shores, distressed European; bless the hour in which thou didst see my verdant fields, my fair navigable rivers, and my green mountains! – If thou wilt work, I have bread for thee; if thou wilt be honest, sober, and industrious, I have greater rewards to confer on thee – ease and independence ... Go thou and work and till; thou shalt prosper, provided thou be just, grateful, and industrious.[5]

The lineaments of the American Dream are all present in these sweeping, rhetorical passages. And soon they will be confirmed, and given permanent expression, in the text of the American Constitution itself. The American Constitution guaranteed all Americans 'life, liberty, and the pursuit of happiness.' This is the heart of the American Dream. In the New World would be created a society dedicated to the ideals of democracy and the rights of men to life, liberty, and the pursuit of happiness. If we recall now that for Fitzgerald American history was 'the history of all aspiration,' 'not just the American dream but the human dream,' then we can recognize that Fitzgerald's understanding transcends the popular trivializing of the American Dream, rather tapping back into the whole cluster of ideas that surrounded the creation of the new American republic. It is of course the ending of *The Great Gatsby* that has come universally to be seen as Fitzgerald's most moving allusion to the original American Dream, but almost as fine is the concluding section of a later story: 'The Swimmers' published in 1929. At the story's end, the protagonist leaves New York for Europe:

> Watching the fading city, the fading shore, from the deck of the Majestic, he had a sense of overwhelming gratitude and gladness that America was there, that under the ugly debris of industry the rich land still pushed up, incorrigibly lavish and fertile, and that in the heart of the leaderless people the old generosities and devotions fought on, breaking out sometimes in fanaticism and excess, but indomitable and undefeated.

America was not ultimately merely 'a bizarre accident, a sort of historical sport;' rather, 'the best of America was the best of the world.' And Henry Marston goes on to try to define the distinctiveness of America,

[5]See J. Hector St John de Crèvecoeur, *Letters from an American Farmer* (New York, 1957). (The passages quoted are from 'Introductory Letter' (pp. 7–8), and Letter III 'What is an American' (pp. 40, 63–64).)

as opposed to the old countries of Europe:

> France was a land, England was a people, but America, having about
> it still that quality of the idea, was harder to utter – it was the graves
> at Shiloh and the tired, drawn, nervous faces of its great men, and the
> country boys dying in the Argonne for a phrase that was empty before
> their bodies withered. It was a willingness of the heart.[6]

Like Carraway's 'fragment of lost words', America, with its 'quality of
the idea,' may be 'harder to utter' but Fitzgerald's fiction nonetheless is
a kind of commentary on America and the idea of America that is the
American Dream. Hence if it is true – as has been regularly argued in
the past – that Fitzgerald's work is a unique celebration of failure, then
the failure in question is less personal than social and political. Not so
much the failure of Fitzgerald himself as the failure of the real America
to begin to fulfil the promises of the American Dream. And this is the
theme that continues to fascinate Fitzgerald's readers everywhere.

Such a view, however, is not characteristic of most biographical
and critical accounts of Fitzgerald which have emphasized his lack of
detachment or self-awareness, his absorption into the world around
him and his struggle for success within it. Fitzgerald's fictional
preoccupation with such themes as failure, defeat, and loss, have
been seen not as looking outward to a society and a history, to
which he belongs, but rather as looking inward to his own sense
of personal frustration and failure. If there is any larger connection
between Fitzgerald and his times, then the standard view is that it is
a purely symbiotic one. Oscar Wilde wrote in 'De Profundis' that he
stood 'in symbolic relations to the art and culture' of his own time:
this is exactly how most commentators have seen Fitzgerald. From all
the excitement of his early success, and the fast and furious pace of his
life thereafter, all the way down to the bitterness and frustration of his
final crack-up, Fitzgerald's life and career have been seen as a tragic
mirror of the historical realities of Jazz Age America in its destructive
movement from boom to bust. What such accounts imply of course
is that Fitzgerald was so absorbed in, so caught up by the hectic life
of 1920s America that he became their history. He not only invented
Jazz Age America but lived it. Yet *The Last Tycoon* note on American
history suggests a very different Fitzgerald: seeing himself as coming at
the end of the American Dream but still occupying a place in the line
of pioneers, he seems to stand outside history, observing, looking on,

---

[6]F. Scott and Zelda Fitzgerald, *Bits of Paradise* (Penguin Books, 1976), pp. 190–191.

not blindly caught up. This contrast or ambivalence – because I accept the view that Fitzgerald was much of the time totally absorbed by the 1920s, the age which, as he wrote 'bore him up, flattered him and gave him more money than he had dreamed of' – is crucially important.[7] It takes us to the very heart of Fitzgerald's position as a writer. All his life, Fitzgerald struggled to reconcile conflicting demands: the demands of life, on the one hand, of art on the other. Fitzgerald was committed to being a writer – his sense of professional vocation was tremendously powerful – but he was also committed, particularly after his marriage to Zelda, to a particular kind of life. As a writer, he felt the need to stand back, to observe, to look on at life – his own life, his life with Zelda, his friends, New York, America, Europe, everything he saw and did and felt – but as a man he needed to give himself unreservedly to all these things. The result was a tension that he never found a way of finally resolving. Hardly surprisingly that tension, so apparent in Fitzgerald's everyday life, surfaces as a unifying theme in the body of his fiction – as I hope to show in subsequent chapters. At this point I should like to glance at Fitzgerald's biography as a way of perhaps identifying the sources of the crucial tension or conflict I have described.

II

In terms of his career as a writer, the most important moment in Fitzgerald's life was his marriage to Zelda Sayre of Alabama. Late in his life, Fitzgerald himself agreed that this was so. In 1938, writing to his daughter at a time when he was worried by her irresponsible behaviour at school, he explained in the most explicit terms just how fateful the decision to marry Zelda had been:

> When I was your age I lived with a great dream. The dream grew and I learned how to speak of it and make people listen. Then the dream divided one day when I decided to marry your mother after all, even though I knew she was spoiled and meant no good to me. I was sorry immediately I had married her but, being patient in those days, made the best of it and got to love her in another way.... But I was a man divided – she wanted me to work too much for **her** and not enough for my dream. She realized too late that work was dignity, and the only dignity, and tried to atone for it by working herself, but it was too late

[7]See 'Echoes of the Jazz Age' in *The Crack-Up with other Pieces and Stories* (Penguin Books, 1965), p. 9.

and she broke and is broken forever.

It was too late also for me to recoup the damage – I had spent most of my resources, spiritual and material, on her, but I struggled on for five years till my health collapsed, and all I cared about was drink and forgetting.[8]

Of course it is possible to read this letter as no more than an exercise in self-indulgence and self-pity: Fitzgerald blaming Zelda for his own weaknesses and failure. But rather more does seem to be involved. I would suggest that the notion of the divided dream here does precisely pinpoint an internal division that had always marked Fitzgerald. Marriage to Zelda was the fulfilment of one kind of dream – but that dream had nothing to do with the other dream of which Fitzgerald had learned to speak in such a way as to make others listen. Marriage to Zelda, in other words, had nothing to do with his life and career as a writer. After his marriage, Fitzgerald tells Scottie, he had become a divided man: now he had two commitments – one to Zelda, one to the 'dream' which was his writing, and these two were mutually destructive. Another letter to his daughter, written two years later, contains a kind of gloss on the division in his life that Fitzgerald is recognizing here. Following up the notion of the redemptive power of work, Fitzgerald wrote:

> What little I've accomplished has been by the most laborious and uphill work, and I wish now I'd *never* relaxed or looked back – but said at the end of *The Great Gatsby*: 'I've found my line – from now on this comes first. This is my immediate duty – without this I am nothing. . . .'[9]

But the point of course is that Fitzgerald failed utterly to follow up and build on the success of *Gatsby*; his writing was never able to come unequivocally first, or become his 'immediate duty.' However much he may have regretted it looking back, the truth was that the kind of single-minded dedication to his art that is implied here was never possible for him. The divisions ran too deep. He had a commitment to Zelda, to life, as powerful as his commitment to art. Indeed in identifying the source of his problem exclusively with Zelda, Fitzgerald is almost certainly letting himself off too lightly. The impulse to marry Zelda did not come out of thin air; in a sense the marriage was everything he wanted. In other words there had been something in Fitzgerald from the beginning that had yearned exactly for what

[8]Andrew Turnbull, *The Letters of F. Scott Fitzgerald* (Penguin Books, 1968), p. 47.
[9]Turnbull, *Op. cit*, p. 95.

marriage to Zelda seemed to afford him: a kind of social triumphalism. This I think is what the pattern of his early life confirms.

III

What is striking about the young Fitzgerald is that he had a romantic yearning for success and the glamour that went with it; in a sense he may be said to have pursued what I have earlier described as a vulgarized version of the American Dream. Whatever the context, Fitzgerald wanted to stand out, to be one of the best; at the Newman School in New Jersey, and subsequently at Princeton University, he struggled to make his mark, to be known and admired and popular. Academic achievement alone would never have been enough – in fact Fitzgerald's performance as a student was far from outstanding – but success in sport was another matter. Fitzgerald would have loved to have been a football star, but modest success at Newman came to nothing in the tougher world of Princeton football. So the only way for him to make his name at Princeton was through the writing skills which he had already exercised with success at Newman and his earlier school back home in St Paul. And in fact such success as he did achieve at Princeton came only from his writing: his contributions to the *Princeton Tiger*, the *Nassau Literary Magazine*, and the prestigious *Triangle Club* in particular. The *Triangle Club* toured each year with a student-written and produced theatrical show. Fitzgerald's contributions to the Club were so successful that in his Junior Year he was in line to be elected President of the Club: an appointment that would at last have made him a Big Man on campus. However, his academic grades were so poor, that he was disqualified from holding such an office. (When Fitzgerald left Princeton in 1917 to become an officer in the United States army, he had still not fulfilled all the requirements for graduation.)

Nonetheless, Fitzgerald was not a failure at Princeton. Given his Middle-Western background and the relatively modest social status of his parents – characteristically Fitzgerald always seems to have admired his father, something of a Southern gentleman if a less than successful businessman, more than his wealthier, if rather plain, mother – and given too that he had not attended one of the more fashionable East Coast prep schools, Fitzgerald had had to make his way in the University's highly exclusive student world very much on the basis of his own personality and abilities. Perhaps it was this that produced within him a degree of self-conscious realism, even cynicism, about the kind of social standing he sought. But such ambivalent feelings never led him to repudiate the campus values of Princeton. And in the end he achieved most of what he desired. Success in terms of social status at Princeton was very much a question of which eating club one belonged to: Fitzgerald was accepted by Cottage Club, one of the more highly placed in the local hierarchy. Again as a Princeton undergraduate Fitzgerald enjoyed considerable prestige at home in St Paul: on vacation he brought something of the romantic glamour of the East Coast Ivy League university to the routine social life of the Middle Western city, and he was much sought after at dances and parties.

What is clear in all of this is that, with whatever reservations, Fitzgerald was broadly prepared to accept the social values of the world in which he lived. Even if he knew that as a Middle-Westerner, with an Irish Catholic background, he was inevitably something of an outsider in the more exclusive circles of wealthy East Coast society, he was nonetheless determined to make his way within such circles. He had wanted to go to Princeton because he felt that university possessed a special quality of romantic glamour and social prestige. Leaving Princeton, he wanted to look forward to a way of life which possessed the same characteristics.

Having completed his training as an army officer, Fitzgerald was posted in June, 1918, to Camp Sheridan near Montgomery, Alabama. It was in Montgomery that he met the eighteen year old Zelda Sayre. Zelda's father was a judge of the Alabama Supreme Court, her mother, who had artistic leanings, was the daughter of a Kentucky senator. The family, though not wealthy, was thus highly respected in social terms. By the time Fitzgerald met her, Zelda had already established herself as one of the most popular and most talked about young girls in and beyond Montgomery. She was beautiful, lively, headstrong, already behaving with the kind of freedom that would characterize the 'flappers' of the 1920s. Rather like Fitzgerald himself, she was in search of a life of glamour and excitement and success. Within a few weeks of meeting her, Zelda became the focus of all of Fitzgerald's romantic yearnings. Marriage to her would embody the personal and social success he sought. But after their engagement the relationship was never an easy one. On his discharge from the United States army, in February, 1919, Fitzgerald went to New York to work in an advertising agency. Visiting Zelda in Montgomery on several occasions, he found her increasingly reluctant to commit herself to marrying him. Finally in June, 1919, Zelda broke off their engagement. Basically the problem was financial: an aspiring writer, whose first novel, written while he was in the army, had been rejected by the publishers, earning very little in a job he disliked, Fitzgerald was in no position to offer Zelda the kind of life she yearned for. She would not marry a man who was not a success. Ironically it was Fitzgerald's art that saved the day. Later in 1919 the New York publishers Scribners accepted the revised version of his first novel, now entitled *This Side of Paradise*. About the same time, the first of his short stories began to appear in *The Smart Set* and *The Saturday Evening Post*. Fitzgerald's career as a writer, that is, was successfully launched. Early in 1920 the engagement to Zelda was renewed, and their marriage took place in New York in April, 1920, exactly a week after the publication of *This Side of Paradise*. But Fitzgerald never forgot that Zelda had turned him down because he was poor, that he had had to win her back by being successful. In all the sweetness of marriage that element of bitterness remained. Nonetheless, marriage to Zelda, added to the popular success of *This Side of Paradise*, meant that Fitzgerald had apparently achieved his dream. The recognition that in fact his dream was now irrevocably divided between his life and his art would only come later.

2

This Side of Paradise

I

Fitzgerald's current status as one of the classic authors of modern literature is indisputable. All his work is kept continuously in print; the sales of his books are enormous; all students and critics of American literature pay close attention to him. 'Jazz Age America', the version of the American 1920s that he did so much to create, has become permanently etched on our modern consciousness. Yet however secure Fitzgerald's reputation appears to be, questions remain. What is the basis of this reputation? Which individual works are we invited to admire? Which are the classic texts? Even asking these questions makes one aware of the apparent paradox that agreement over Fitzgerald's major status as a writer is not matched by any general agreement that he produced major works.

As early as 1945 – when the revival of interest in Fitzgerald was scarcely underway – William Troy wrote a seminal critical article entitled 'Scott Fitzgerald – the Authority of Failure.'[1] Its burden was that the theme of failure was so powerful in Fitzgerald's fiction that it represented a major source of imaginative strength, but Mr Troy was careful to insist that this in no way meant that Fitzgerald himself was a failure as a writer. Not at all: 'he has left one short novel, passages in several others, and a handful of short stories which stand as much chance of survival as anything of their kind produced in this country

[1]Troy's article was originally published in *Accent*, 1945. It has been reprinted in Alfred Kazin, ed., *F. Scott Fitzgerald: The Man and his Work* (New York, 1951) and in Arthur Mizener, *F. Scott Fitzgerald: A Collection of Critical Essays* (Englewood Cliffs, New Jersey, 1963).

during the same period.' Nearly half a century on, this list hardly strikes one as a definition of success. One short novel, only *passages* in several others, and the odd short story, hardly adds up to the canon of a major author. One feels that Fitzgerald's reputation ought to be more securely founded than this meagre list allows.

Yet what is even stranger is that in the decades that have followed 1945, when Fitzgerald's lost reputation has been restored and indeed carried to new heights, little has happened to make William Troy's assessment seem particularly eccentric. The great majority of critics seem broadly to continue to share his view. The number of works by Fitzgerald universally seen as critically successful remains remarkably few. Only *The Great Gatsby* (1925) of the novels is seen as an – almost – unqualified success. For the rest, the conventional critical opinion is surprisingly uniform. The first two novels, *This Side of Paradise* (1920) and *The Beautiful and Damned* (1922) are invariably dismissed as early, immature, apprentice works, hardly worth serious critical consideration. *Tender is the Night* (1934), too long in the writing, is structurally flawed, its themes inadequately understood by its author, while *The Last Tycoon* (1941) is at best no more than a promising fragment of a novel. As far as the short stories are concerned, a few such as 'May Day', 'Babylon Revisited', and 'the Rich Boy' have been widely admired, but the great majority are seen, as Fitzgerald himself saw them, as material produced to meet their author's constant need for a quick financial return.

Such a record compels one to ask whether there is any other major author who has written so little that has been accorded general critical acclaim. Nor is there a case here of an author succeeding in alternative forms of writing. Fitzgerald's one play, *The Vegetable* (1923) was a failure. His film scripts for Hollywood were poorly received. Only a handful of autobiographical essays could be seen as adding to his reputation. Yet despite all this one's sense of Fitzgerald's importance as a writer remains; the flawed aspects of individual works do not in the end seem that important. Fitzgerald, as we have seen, not only survives but flourishes. The author adds up to something substantially more than the sum of the individual parts. How could such a situation arise? Two answers are possible, and both suggest that the problem lies less with Fitzgerald than with his critics.

II

The first answer relates to the extraordinary status that has been gained by *The Great Gatsby*. Because the other novels are not *Gatsby*, they are failures. Before the achievement of *Gatsby* the received critical wisdom is of course that Fitzgerald was still learning how to write a novel: *This Side of Paradise* and *The Beautiful and Damned* are apprentice works at best. After *Gatsby*, Fitzgerald lost his way and thus failed to repeat *Gatsby*'s success. The assumption behind all of this is that Fitzgerald aimed always at what he achieved perfectly only once – in *The Great Gatsby*. But this in fact is not the case. Fitzgerald knew perfectly well that *Gatsby* did not provide a model for all of his fiction. His own view was that he had chosen to write two quite different types of novel – even if on occasion he used slightly different terms to distinguish between them. Thus in a 1933 letter to the writer John Peale Bishop, a friend since undergraduate days at Princeton, he called *The Great Gatsby* a 'dramatic' novel while *Tender is the Night* was a 'philosophical, now called psychological' one. To compare the two, he wrote, would be like 'comparing a sonnet sequence with an epic.'[2] The difference is further explicated in a Hollywood letter of 1937. His novels, wrote Fitzgerald, 'have alternated between being selective and blown up. *Paradise* and *Gatsby* were selective; *The Beautiful and Damned* and *Tender* aimed at being full and comprehensive.' 'In *This Side of Paradise* (in a crude way) and in *Gatsby*,' he went on, 'I selected the stuff to fit a given mood or "hauntedness" or whatever you might call it. . . .'[3] *The Beautiful and Damned* and *Tender is the Night*, that is, deliberately include the fullness and range of detail the other two novels omit. The point then is clearly made that *Gatsby*, whatever its success, was not seen by Fitzgerald as providing a single model for the writing of a novel. But just as some critics were disappointed that *The Beautiful and Damned*, so radically different in tone and mood, did not attempt to follow up the popular success of *This Side of Paradise*, so others regretted that *Tender is the Night* was written in a form quite unlike that of *Gatsby*. On both occasions Fitzgerald was determined to do something different; his critics, however, looked to him to do something much the same.

Of course one must concede that there is a possibility that the critics were right: perhaps the more dramatic kind of novel was indeed Fitzgerald's strength. He should have had the aesthetic self-awareness to recognize this and continue with it. But there is another point of view. Unquestionably the highly economical 'selectiveness' of *Gatsby*

[2]Andrew Turnbull, ed., *The Letters of F. Scott Fitzgerald* (Penguin Books, 1968), p. 383.
[3]Turnbull, *Op. cit*, p. 571.

does help to explain its jewel-like perfection; but the greater density of detail and emotional fullness of *Tender is the Night* do add to its power to engage and move. Earlier, when *The Beautiful and Damned* was being published, Fitzgerald seemed to blame himself for having 'devoted so much more care ... to the *detail* of the book' than to 'thinking out the *general* scheme;' but he was quite wrong to do so.[4] General schemes – philosophical, political, social or whatever – were never Fitzgerald's strength. In a 1936 letter to Max Perkins, contrasting himself with General Grant, about whom he had been reading, he wrote: 'What attitude on life I have been able to put into my books is dependent upon entirely different field of reference with the predominant themes based on problems of personal psychology.'[5] 'Personal psychology' rather than any 'general scheme' is invariably Fitzgerald's starting-point. His movement is always from the individual outward to the wider social issue of whatever kind. Thus the strength of *The Beautiful and Damned* lies precisely in its density of detail, emotional and psychological, rather than in any grandly philosophical or interpretative scheme.

The second explanation I would offer for Fitzgerald's simultaneous existence as a successful and failed author involves the early establishment of a critical tradition concerning his work which consistently undervalued and patronized him. From the beginning of his career, Fitzgerald had all the wrong credentials for being accepted as a great artist and writer. Attending Princeton – which he described as 'the pleasantest country club in America,' – he had chosen the wrong, too glamorous, university. As a young man, he was regarded as strikingly handsome, and in marrying Zelda Sayre he allied himself with a Southern beauty, however unconventional. Soon the brightest of bright young couples had acquired a flashy reputation for their expensive lifestyle and avid pursuit of pleasure and happiness. Fitzgerald took up no fashionable political cause. Most importantly of all, however, he achieved literary fame and popular success at an incredibly early age. Youth, beauty, success – has such a combination ever been warmly greeted by critics? (Probably Fitzgerald's one stroke of good fortune in his life was being a man.)

The critical answer to the Fitzgerald phenomenon was the creation – whether entirely consciously or not does not matter – of a perspective on Fitzgerald as a writer that has never ceased to dominate critical thinking about him. The fact that Fitzgerald himself tended to go

[4]Turnbull, *Op. cit*, p. 373.
[5]Turnbull, *Op. cit*, p. 289.

along with crucial aspects of this perspective did nothing at all to lessen the long-term critical damage it caused him. The lineaments of this early-established and continuing critical tradition are as follows. Firstly, Fitzgerald was not to be taken seriously as a conscious artist; his successes originated solely in his 'natural' talent as a gifted writer. Just as the Edinburgh literati in the eighteenth century chose to regard Robert Burns as a 'heaven-taught ploughman,' so American intellectuals in the 1920s regarded Fitzgerald as a kind of inspired ham. Secondly, and consequentially, they regarded Fitzgerald as intellectually weak. His critics were all much cleverer than he was. Some of them would have even remembered how poor his grades were at Princeton. Fitzgerald himself was much inclined to accept this poor estimate of his intellectual ability. In one of the 'Crack-Up' articles in 1936 he wrote that in the last twenty years he 'had done very little thinking, save within the problems of my craft.'[6] As early as 1925 he had told Gertrude Stein that he was 'a very second-rate person compared to first-rate people,'[7] and towards the end of his life, in 1939, he was typically telling Edmund Wilson that he was 'still the ignoramus that you and John Bishop wrote about at Princeton.'[8] Perhaps then it is not surprising that his critics decided that Fitzgerald wrote by instinct and had nothing to say – at least in the sense of ideas to explore or communicate. But there was a third, and still more damaging, strand in the critical argument concerning Fitzgerald's status as a writer. Fitzgerald, it was argued, never lived up to his early promise. And the reason was that he never grew up. His work remained *immature. The Great Gatsby* was allowed to be 'more mature' than *This Side of Paradise* and *The Beautiful and Damned*, but *Tender is the Night* did not sustain the process of maturation. Hence was established the persistent critical tradition that patronizingly wrote off Fitzgerald as a natural but immature writer of limited intellectual weight and understanding.

How did such a view come to be so firmly established? One reason, as I have said, was Fitzgerald's own readiness to go along with much of it. Another was the way in which Fitzgerald's whole personality and way of life struck his more serious-minded contemporaries as incompatible with a creative achievement that demanded to be taken seriously. After all, over and over again Fitzgerald drew his material from that Jazz Age 'smart set' to which he and Zelda belonged. Most critics seem to have found it impossible to believe that such a world

[6]F. Scott Fitzgerald, *The Crack-Up with other Pieces and Stories* (Penguin Books, 1965), p. 49.
[7]Turnbull, *Op. cit*, p. 504.
[8]Turnbull, *Op. cit*, p. 368.

could ever provide material appropriate to the needs of serious and mature fiction. The assumption was that superficial characters in a superficial society could only mean superficial art. Only once, in the 1934 Introduction to the Modern Library edition of *The Great Gatsby*, did Fitzgerald allow himself a moment of protest at such an assumption:

> . . . I had recently been kidded half haywire by critics who felt that my material was such as to preclude all dealing with mature persons in a mature world. But, my God! it was my material, and it was all I had to deal with.

Fitzgerald interestingly picks up the maturity point here, but the problem goes deeper than he is prepared to allow. The difficulty is not just the limited nature of his material, it is how that material is presented. As a man, he is wholly caught up in a 'Jazz Age' way of life, whether in New York, or Paris, or the south of France. How then, as an artist, can he see that life with critical discernment and detachment, and so be regarded seriously as a writer? The problem was compounded by the fact that, as a man, Fitzgerald was all too visible to his contemporaries; he was, as it were, too familiar, too well known. His early critics remembered him as an undergraduate at Princeton, and the Fitzgerald they knew remained just that. The idea that he – and not the Edmund Wilsons or John Peale Bishops – should become the major writer of their generation was never going to be fully acceptable to them: their Fitzgerald inevitably remained the not very clever Scott they had known. His recurring not very clever, or even outrageous, behaviour with Zelda merely confirmed what they knew of him. Hence the tone of easy superiority they adopted in writing about him.

III

I have attempted to explain how the conventional critical wisdom about Fitzgerald's work came into being, and how that critical tradition seemed to endorse the paradox that Fitzgerald was simultaneously a successful and a failed writer. As far as his fiction is concerned, what has been the result? The most obvious one is the very real neglect of the early novels, *This Side of Paradise* and *The Beautiful and Damned*. Both of these have been conventionally labelled as immature works which the reader may reasonably ignore as he or she moves quickly to *The Great Gatsby*. The myth has prevailed, that is, that the early Fitzgerald novels are not worthy of serious critical attention. The truth is rather different.

In any event, what is really extraordinary about the conventional critical view of the early novels is the extent to which it ignores and discounts the experience of Fitzgerald's original readers. They at least did not neglect *This Side of Paradise* and *The Beautiful and Damned*. Like the unbiased reader of today, they read them for what they were: not necessarily great novels, but good all the same, eminently readable, written with verve and style, and containing more than a little psychological and emotional honesty, even if sometimes of a self-contradictory kind. Undoubtedly these early novels had serious flaws – a tendency towards excess, romantic extravagance, name-dropping and an uneasy intellectual pretentiousness – but such flaws were in no way able to deprive the novels of their vivid freshness and appeal. The early readers of *This Side of Paradise* who were electrified by the book, who insisted that their lives were changed by it – the half a million men and women readers between the ages of fifteen and thirty whom John O'Hara tells us fell in love with it[9] – who were sure they were reading a serious novel by a serious novelist: they had it right. They at least were responding to the book just as it was, their reactions unsullied by the subsequent Fitzgerald myth. Similarly those who responded to the bleakness and power of *The Beautiful and Damned* were also correct: certainly more correct than those critics who insisted that the second novel's portrayal of individual disintegration and defeat reflected no more than Fitzgerald's recent reading of the American naturalists like Dreiser and Frank Norris.

Fitzgerald's early novels are full of uncertainties and contradictions. What is wrong, and who is to blame for it, is not always clear; moral ambiguities are more apparent than firm moral judgements. In the early 1920s, this may well have been an important source of the books' appeal. The texts refuse judgement because the author, uncertain himself over what is right and what is wrong, is concerned above all to delineate experience exactly as he perceives it. The truth about life is sought – but not necessarily achieved. Hence the moral absences and ambiguities that have traditionally been seen as damaging flaws. The position is complicated by the obvious contradictions within Fitzgerald himself. It is important to recognize that Fitzgerald is not a product of the 1920s; his roots belong to an older, pre-war America. Hence the moral uncertainties, the loss of

[9]See Bruccoli, *Some Sort of Epic Grandeur*, p. 127.

confidence in traditional values, characteristic of the post-war 20s, were not accepted uncritically by Fitzgerald. Part at least of his temperament involved a quite powerful impulse towards judgement almost puritanical in its nature. He once explained his refusal to become simply a popular entertainer as a result of his desire to 'preach at people in some acceptable form.'

Thus it is easy to find in *This Side of Paradise* and *The Beautiful and Damned* passages or episodes that depend upon or uphold quite conventional moral attitudes. On the other hand, as an artist creating and peopling a fictional world, Fitzgerald allowed other dimensions of his own open responsiveness to life and experience to emerge in what he wrote. The moral censoriousness of which both Amory Blaine in *This Side of Paradise* and Anthony Patch in *The Beautiful and Damned* are capable is never the whole story. In fact it is often the absence of simple moral judgements, the doubts and confusions of the characters, and the sense of being bewildered by the complexities of experience, that give a special kind of life and appeal to the early novels. It is almost certainly true that in these fictions Fitzgerald is often trying to work out his own growing problems in trying to cope with experience; that he finds it difficult to come up with straightforward answers is neither surprising nor necessarily a sign of immaturity or intellectual weakness. A life-long admirer of Keats, Fitzgerald subsequently came to defend such uncertainty in terms very similar to those the romantic poet employed to define his concept of 'negative capability': in *The Crack-Up*, Fitzgerald observed that 'the test of a first-rate intelligence is the ability to hold two opposed ideas in the mind at the same time, and still retain the ability to function.'[10] In a general artistic sense such a capacity had always been present in his fiction, working to qualify the strain of moral puritanism in his temperament.

The non-judgemental, even morally confused, quality that contributes to the success of Fitzgerald's early novels is well-illustrated by a single scene in *This Side of Paradise*. The beautiful Rosalind is struggling to explain why she cannot marry a penniless Amory Blaine. Amory asks whether she intends to marry the wealthy Dawson Ryder.

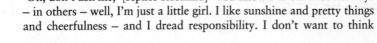

> 'Oh, don't ask me,' [replies Rosalind] 'You know I'm old in some ways
> – in others – well, I'm just a little girl. I like sunshine and pretty things
> and cheerfulness – and I dread responsibility. I don't want to think

[10]*The Crack-Up*, p. 39.

about pots and kitchens and brooms. I want to worry whether my legs
will get slick and brown when I swim in the summer.'[11]

Such an admission is of course overwhelming evidence of Rosalind's
utter selfishness and moral irresponsibility. And indeed this passage
has been adduced as a prime example of how Rosalind comes across
to the reader as a much more essentially superficial character than
Fitzgerald realizes. Yet the passage does resist such a simple judgement. Clearly Rosalind realizes that she is wrong to think and feel
as she does. But she is not prepared to deny the truth. For her,
whether or not her legs are tanned in summer is something that really
matters, and she wants it to go on mattering. Her youth, her beauty,
her desires – these things count, and she is not prepared to gainsay
them. Fitzgerald is not in the business of condemning her for that; like
Amory, he understands Rosalind's need and thus cannot condemn it.
One suspects that it was exactly this kind of understanding, shared
by the novel's youthful audience, that helps to explain its enormous
success.

IV

This Side of Paradise was published in 1920. Fitzgerald had worked
extremely hard to get it into print. The first draft of the novel had
been completed exactly two years earlier when Fitzgerald was a second
lieutenant in the United States army. Then entitled 'The Romantic
Egotist,' the manuscript was submitted to the New York publisher
Scribners who rejected it. Later in 1918, Scribners also rejected a
revised version of the novel. Fitzgerald was discharged from the army
early in 1919. Hoping to marry Zelda in the near future, Fitzgerald
began his job with the advertising agency in New York. But within
weeks, as we have seen in Chapter One, he was forced to face the fact
that Zelda would not marry a poorly paid, still unsuccessful writer.
While his personal life was in turmoil, however, his professional
literary career made its first advance: H.L. Mencken accepted a short
story for his prestigious magazine *The Smart Set*. Encouraged by this,
and driven by the apparent loss of Zelda, Fitzgerald threw up his job
in New York and went home to his parents' house in St Paul to rewrite
his novel once again. The new version was produced over the summer

[11]F. Scott Fitzgerald, *This Side of Paradise* (Penguin Books, 1963), p. 178. All subsequent page references are to this edition.

of 1919 and in September Maxwell Perkins at Scribners accepted it for publication.

When *This Side of Paradise* appeared in March, 1920, it was an immediate success. Its young author became a celebrity overnight. In reply to a critical letter from the President of Princeton, Fitzgerald admitted that his novel had over-accentuated the 'country club' atmosphere of the university – 'It is the Princeton of Saturday night in May'[12] – but in fact the objections of such an establishment figure only go to underline the instant appeal of the book to a younger generation of postwar Americans, uncertain of their commitment to the conservative values of the past. Such little critical attention as the novel has subsequently received has been largely concerned with trying to explain – or explain away – its extraordinary popular appeal.

Various points have been made that are no doubt true. Fitzgerald's novel did succeed in articulating something of the sense of uncertainty about the future, and about how to live in the present, characteristic of at least some sections of American society in the years after World War I. Not all readers may have identified with the hero Amory Blaine, but Amory's recognition that the world he was living in was a new and changing one does seem to have touched a highly sensitive contemporary nerve. When Amory, in the novel's closing paragraphs, meditates on a new generation, learning the old creeds, but 'dedicated more than the last to the fear of poverty and the worship of success' and 'grown up to find all Gods dead, all wars fought, all faiths in man shaken . . .' (p. 253), he seems to have produced a responsive echo in the hearts and minds of countless younger readers. The fact too that the novel focused on college men and college life contributed to its appeal. Like the so-called 'silver fork' Victorian novels, with their putative accounts of the lives of the English aristocracy, the book offered its readers vicarious insight into the way of life of one kind of American élite. Then the novel's formal characteristics, its use of a variety of modes – prose, poetry, dramatized scenes – its headings and sub-headings, borrowed, as Fitzgerald later admitted, from Shaw's Prefaces, must have struck at least some readers as appealingly new and radical and 'modern'.

Ultimately, however, the best explanation of *This Side of Paradise*'s success is simply that it tells a good story in a manner that more than holds the reader's interest. Almost inevitably, given the age at which Fitzgerald wrote it, the novel is very much a *bildungsroman*, charting Amory Blaine's growing up into life and experience. It opens with the

[12]Turnbull, *Op. cit*, p. 483.

young Amory moving to Minneapolis, shifts quickly to prep school in New England, then to Princeton University in New Jersey, just south of New York, and finally to New York city in the immediate post-First World War period. The novel is relatively short, and it lacks any developing complexity of plot or theme. In terms of form and structure too it is episodic, held together only by the constant presence of its protagonist whose various experiences it narrates. The nature of these experiences is best suggested by the fact that the major portion of the book concerns Amory's university life at Princeton. *This Side of Paradise* is one of the original campus novels.

Despite his sense of his own uniqueness, and the splendid destiny that awaits him, Amory Blaine comes across as a kind of archetypal undergraduate. Alert, interested, enthusiastic, responding eagerly to new knowledge and ideas, struggling to think things out for himself, he is simultaneously vain, egotistical and self-indulgent. With his fellow-students (all male) he constantly debates issues and ideas involving religion, society, politics and life in general; recent and contemporary literature is another recurring theme. But all of this undergraduate theorizing co-exists with a preoccupation with the romantic world of girls and sexuality. In fact, Amory's emotional equilibrium is constantly at the mercy of the success or failure of his personal relationships. And in the course of the novel it is mainly failure that he experiences. With Isabelle, Rosalind, and Eleanor in turn Amory comes to grief. All three girls are dazzlingly beautiful and desirably attractive, but in each case Amory discovers that they are even more vain and coldly self-centred than he is.

This Side of Paradise remains fascinating today partly because of the insight it provides into the new mores and life-style of a privileged class of Americans in the immediate postwar period. But what is equally interesting is Amory Blaine's own ambivalence about the new permissiveness he observes around him. He at least respects older codes of conduct and it comes as no surprise when, at one of the novel's climaxes, he heroically, if cynically, sacrifices his own good name to preserve that of a friend in a seedy affair involving girls in a hotel in Atlantic City. Amory's spiritual and moral mentor is Monsignor Darcy, a sophisticated and worldly Roman Catholic cleric, and Amory clearly finds the idea of a Catholic religious faith attractive, even if it remains out of reach. Perhaps this is why some of his harsher youthful experiences convince him of the reality and power of evil, which he comes to associate with beauty and sexuality.

The reader undoubtedly finds it easy to sympathize with Amory in the confusions and contradictions of his attitudes, hopes and feelings, but the strength of *This Side of Paradise* does not really lie in the depth of its characterization or the profundity of its themes. Rather it exists in the qualities of freshness and exuberance, in the novel and its writing, which allows Amory Blaine's thoughts and feelings, however youthfully 'undergraduate' they may be, to be communicated to the reader with an appealing vividness and clarity.

Inevitably Fitzgerald was made dizzy by the success of *This Side of Paradise*. By the end of 1921 the novel had sold just under fifty thousand copies: an excellent figure for a first novel, but not enough to make it a real bestseller. (Sinclair Lewis's *Main Street*, also published in 1920, sold 295,000 copies.) Fitzgerald's royalties were not on a scale to make him rich, but his financial position nonetheless seemed transformed. The poor boy had made good. Later he wrote that in 1919 his writing had earned him eight hundred dollars; in 1920 that figure had become eighteen thousand dollars.[13] Less happily, what the success of *This Side of Paradise* did was to create in Fitzgerald expectations about his future work in terms of sales and money which were destined never to be realized: despite the critical acclaim with which *The Great Gatsby* would be received, *This Side of Paradise* remained his most popular book. On the question of how good a novel it was, Fitzgerald in later years came characteristically to share the views of those of his critics who were all too willing to emphasize the book's obvious weaknesses. No doubt, as I have noted, *This Side of Paradise* is uneven, structurally loose, and some of the time sentimental and self-indulgent. Its large debts to Fitzgerald's undergraduate reading have always been recognized: all of Fitzgerald's favourite authors are drawn upon, from Compton Mackenzie and Booth Tarkington to Wells and Henry Adams. Fitzgerald himself once called the novel 'A Romance and a Reading List' and the joke is well-taken: the undergraduate characters are much given to literary name-dropping. (One scholar has worked out that the text mentions sixty-four titles and ninety-eight writers.) Yet Fitzgerald was never prepared to dismiss the book entirely. In 1925 he wrote in his personal copy:

> I like this book for the enormous emotion, mostly immature and bogus, that gives every incident a sort of silly 'life.'[14]

What was most bogus, he correctly decided, was the fourth and final of Amory Blaine's adventures with women. Of the Eleanor episode

[13]See 'Early Success' in *The Crack-Up with other Pieces and Stories*, p. 61.
[14]See Bruccoli, *Some Sort of Epic Grandeur*, p. 122.

Fitzgerald wrote: 'This is so funny I can't even bear to read it.'[15] Even as late as 1938, his general view of the book had not changed significantly. In a letter of that year he wrote:

> Looking it over, I think it is now one of the funniest books since *Dorian Gray* in its utter spuriousness – and then, here and there, I find a page that is very real and living.[16]

Perhaps these are the pages he had in mind when he said later in the same year that he had written in the novel of 'a love affair that was still bleeding as fresh as the skin wound on a haemophile.'[17]

Fitzgerald's criticisms of *This Side of Paradise* exemplify one of his major problems as a writer: an altogether too deferential regard for the opinions of his contemporary critics. Fitzgerald seems to have lacked the intellectual and artistic self-confidence to stand up for himself and answer back. It is entirely characteristic of him to reply to a letter from Gertrude Stein, praising *This Side of Paradise*, in wholly negative and self-deprecatory terms. Having described himself as a 'very second-rate person' he continues, 'it honestly makes me shiver to know that such a writer as you attributes such a significance to my factitious, meretricious *This Side of Paradise*.'[18] Yet presumably it was qualities other than its factitiousness and meretriciousness that made John O'Hara's half a million youthful readers fall in love with the book. Alfred Kazin has written that Fitzgerald 'is easier to appreciate than to explain' and that is particularly true of his first novel.[19] For all its obvious faults, *This Side of Paradise* remains a surprisingly fresh and lively text. It merits readers rather than condescension.

V

There is another reason why *This Side of Paradise* deserves attention. When it is read less as a self-contained, autonomous work than as an opening statement in Fitzgerald's career as a novelist, then it reveals further significant levels of meaning. The decision to write and re-write *This Side of Paradise* involved crucial aspects of Fitzgerald's life; successful completion and publication of the novel would on the

---

[15]Bruccoli, *Some Sort of Epic Grandeur*, p. 125.
[16]Turnbull, *Op. cit*, p. 297.
[17]Turnbull, *Op. cit*, p. 598.
[18]Turnbull, *Op. cit*, p. 504.
[19]Kazin, ed., *F. Scott Fitzgerald: The Man and His Work*, p. 17.

one hand establish his credentials as a professional writer; on the other, the decision to persevere with the writing of the novel was clearly a reaction to the broken engagement with Zelda. The writing of a successful novel was the only way in which he could be in a position to win her back. Thus pressures from both art and life are at work on the novel. Writing *This Side of Paradise* Fitzgerald was attempting to do two things: he was seeking to discover the kind of writer he wanted to be, but he was also exploring the kind of man he was. To find a satisfactory and satisfying definition of himself as man and writer was destined to remain a central problem for the rest of his life. Not surprisingly, given its importance in his career, it is a theme that constantly surfaces in his fiction. The problem was that all too often the roles of man and writer seemed to pull in opposite directions. As a professional writer, Fitzgerald felt the need to be detached and objective, the disciplined observer of life and experience; as a man, however, particularly after his marriage to Zelda in April 1920, he felt himself totally committed to the fullness of living, without restraint or discrimination, both using and being used by life in all its aspects. The result was an extraordinary tension between the demands of art and the demands of life that Fitzgerald was never able fully to resolve.

The point of course is not that *This Side of Paradise* is 'about' this tension. *This Side of Paradise* is simply the story of Amory Blaine and the various difficulties and problems, emotional and intellectual, he experiences as a young man at Princeton. But there is nonetheless a kind of subtext within which the issue I see as central to Fitzgerald's career as a writer does emerge. Amory is a writer, or at least a potential writer. He has one 'cynical' short story published but he decides he has too much concern for the 'responsibilities of authorship' to go on writing. He has just finally lost Rosalind, and in the state of emotional collapse that follows, seems to regard writing and the life of the mind as no more than substitutes for the 'life' that Rosalind had embodied:

> There seemed suddenly to be much left in life, if only this revival of old interests did not mean that he was backing away from it again – backing away from life itself. (p. 191)

Recalling himself at the end of the war as 'the heart-whole boy who had stepped off the transport, passionately desiring the adventure of life,' (p. 198) and despite the fact that the Rosalind adventure has caused him nothing but pain, Amory is still afraid that art can only be pursued at the expense of life. Talking with his friend Tom about what to do with his life in the post-Rosalind situation, he is advised to 'try fiction.' But he rejects the suggestion:

> 'Trouble is I get distracted when I start to write stories – get afraid
> I'm doing it instead of living – get thinking maybe life is waiting for me
> in the Japanese gardens at the Ritz or at Atlantic City or on the lower
> East Side.' (p. 195)

Clearly for Amory art and life are mutually exclusive.

However, it is in the closing pages of *This Side of Paradise* that the issues emerge most directly. The context is Amory Blaine's car ride towards Princeton during which he argues the case for socialism with a wealthy industrialist and his secretary. Traditional criticism has tended to disparage the episode, arguing that there has been no preparation for Amory's sudden espousal of socialist principles. But the strength of the episode is exactly its unexpectedness and inconclusiveness: Amory – like Fitzgerald – is in the process of working something out for himself, and the answers he arrives at are no more than tentative. In the course of the argument, Amory, attempting to discriminate between the social attitudes of different categories of people, develops the notion of the 'spiritually married man.' What is so significant here is the way in which marriage becomes a metaphor for entrapment in the social status quo; the spiritually married person has lost his independence, can no longer afford to be neutral or objective or dispassionate – 'Life's got him,' (p. 244) as the text beautifully puts it. To remain free, to be in a position to work for change, to be any kind of radical – and writers may fall into that category – it is essential to remain 'unmarried.' But the point is that Amory Blaine's ambitions throughout most of *This Side of Paradise* push him in precisely the opposite direction: 'success' at school and university, and still more the fulfilment of his romantic, emotional yearnings, involve above all a commitment to things, a surrender of the self to others. And Fitzgerald himself is about to become a literally married man. After attending the funeral of Monsignor Darcy, his former spiritual mentor, Amory believes he comes to a new understanding of himself and what he wants: not to be admired, not to be loved, 'but to be necessary to people, to be indispensable.' Amory 'felt an immense desire to give people a sense of security.' (p. 239) The real question is whether such a desire is compatible with the 'unmarried' stance of detachment required of the true artist. Again, Amory decides that his experience with women has led him to recognize a link between beauty and evil. As a result he concludes that he can never become the kind of artist who is dedicated above all to the pursuit of beauty:

He felt that he was leaving behind him his chance of being a certain type of artist. It seemed so much more important to be a certain sort of man. (p. 252)

Once again the unresolved question for Fitzgerald was whether being that sort of man was in the end compatible with remaining the spiritually unmarried artist.

3

The Beautiful and Damned

I

The Beautiful and Damned, Fitzgerald's second novel, was published in March, 1922, exactly two years after *This Side of Paradise*. It remains easily Fitzgerald's most neglected book. Writing the Fitzgerald chapter in the 1978 *American Literary Scholarship* volume, Jackson R. Bryer refers correctly to it as 'this strangely sprawling and bitter novel which has been, for the most part, ignored by critics.'[1] Such neglect has almost nothing to do with the novel's literary merit. Rather what it reflects is the enduring power of the critical tradition that insists that Fitzgerald's early novels are immature, apprentice works. In fact the occasion of one of the key sources in the establishing of that tradition was the appearance of *The Beautiful and Damned*. In the *Bookman* for March, 1922, Edmund Wilson wrote a long article on Fitzgerald's work which rehearsed the familiar arguments about Fitzgerald being a gifted writer who unfortunately lacked intellectual power and control and thus had nothing very interesting to say.[2]

The tone of Wilson's piece is nicely set by its opening allusion to comments on Fitzgerald allegedly made by Edna St Vincent Millay after meeting him in Paris. Millay is supposed to have said that to meet Fitzgerald is to think of a stupid old woman who has been left a diamond – the woman is proud of the diamond and shows it to everyone, but everyone is quite surprised that such an ignorant

[1]See J. Albert Robbins, ed., *American Literary Scholarship* (1978) (Durham, North Carolina, 1980), p. 170.
[2]Wilson's article is reprinted in Arthur Mizener, ed., *F. Scott Fitzgerald: A Collection of Critical Essays* (Englewood Cliffs, New Jersey, 1963), pp. 80–85.

old woman should possess such a jewel, which she can talk about only in the most inept manner. Wilson allows that this is hardly an accurate picture of Scott Fitzgerald, but immediately insists that 'there **is** a symbolic truth in the description.' It is true, he tells us, because Fitzgerald 'has been given imagination without intellectual control of it; he has been given the desire for beauty without an aesthetic ideal; and he has been given a gift for expression without very many ideas to express.' Given such an opening, Wilson's less than enthusiastic account of *The Beautiful and Damned*, and all of Fitzgerald's earlier writing, comes as no surprise. *This Side of Paradise* is allowed life – gaiety and colour and movement; but 'it has almost every fault and deficiency that a novel can possibly have.' It 'commits almost every sin that a novel can possibly commit.' It is a 'preposterous farrago,' and it is 'very immaturely imagined.' The novel is indeed well-written, but 'well-written in spite of its illiteracies.' Fitzgerald's other works fare little better. Towards the end of his article, Wilson suggests that Fitzgerald's 'restless imagination may yet produce something durable,' but at present this imagination 'suffers badly from lack of discipline and poverty of aesthetic ideas' – even his stories 'have a way of petering out.' Finally, *The Beautiful and Damned*, 'imperfect though it is,' is allowed to represent an advance over *This Side of Paradise*: 'the style is more nearly mature and the subject more solidly unified, and there are scenes that are more convincing than any in his previous fiction.' But the tone throughout Wilson's article remains superior and condescending.

Edmund Wilson did have the decency to send Fitzgerald a copy of his article before publication. Amazingly, but all too characteristically, Fitzgerald was enthusiastic. He told Wilson that he took 'an extra-ordinary delight' in the article's 'considered approbation' and that he 'enjoyed it enormously.' What he did ask Wilson to do was to omit from his draft all references to his drinking, and he suggests that in listing influences upon him Wilson was wrong to omit Zelda:

> '– the most enormous influence on me in the four and a half years since I met her has been the complete, fine and full-hearted selfishness and chill-mindedness of Zelda.'[3]

Despite the fact that the article did eventually lead to some ill-feeling between the two friends, Fitzgerald remained convinced that Wilson

---

[3]Andrew Turnbull, ed., *The Letters of F. Scott Fitzgerald* (Penguin Books, 1968), pp. 350–51.

had done him a favour by writing it. His first reaction was that 'the article ought to be in my favor;'[4] and even after falling out over details, he told Wilson he was 'immensely grateful' to him for having done it.[5] In fact Fitzgerald was quite wrong. The article damaged his reputation. It did nothing to persuade other critics to take him seriously as an artist, and it encouraged the notion that his work was immature. When exactly 'maturity' emerged in accepted critical vocabulary as a term of praise is not clear. Nor it is self-evident what is meant when a piece of writing is described as 'mature': except presumably that more is meant than that the author is over forty. However it is clear that to be called 'mature' is a good thing, whereas to be labelled 'immature' is highly damaging. Given that Fitzgerald had two novels published by the time he was twenty-five it was more or less inevitable that they should be immediately dubbed immature.

In fact Fitzgerald's literary precociousness was not at all un-characteristic of the 1920s in general. The postwar generation does seem to have matured earlier than most. John Dos Passos published his first novel when he was scarcely twenty-four – and he had published another three before he was thirty. Both Faulkner and Hemingway were still in their twenties when their first novels appeared. More significantly, perhaps, Edmund Wilson himself was well under thirty when he wrote his *Bookman* article on Fitzgerald. No doubt there was a sense in which Wilson was cleverer than Fitzgerald; whether he was necessarily more mature is a much more open question.

What is now not in question is that *The Beautiful and Damned* in no way merits neglect. It is a remarkable book. And what is most remarkable about it is how different it is from *This Side of Paradise*. The obvious thing for Fitzgerald to have done – and this presumably is what many readers and critics expected him to do – was to follow up the success of *This Side of Paradise* with another of the same. But this is exactly what he chose not to do. In terms of mood and tone and atmosphere *This Side of Paradise* and *The Beautiful and Damned* could not be more different. Amory Blaine's life in *This Side of Paradise* has its share of failures and disappointments – but the mood remains positive and optimistic; life is full of promise and potential even if the individual has to struggle to win through. Such optimism has disappeared from *The Beautiful and Damned*: life is now a struggle which the individual loses. The tone is correspondingly bleak. Yet despite this contrast, something of the power of *The*

---

[4]Turnbull, *Op. cit*, p. 352.
[5]Turnbull, *Op. cit*, p. 353.

Beautiful and Damned derives from the existence of *This Side of Paradise*. The second novel is very much about the loss of paradise, and as Proust suggested, '*les seuls vrais paradis sont les paradis qu'on a perdus.*'[6] When he was writing *The Beautiful and Damned* Fitzgerald seems to have become increasingly aware that whatever paradise Amory Blaine had yearned for was already beyond recall; Anthony Patch's experience in the second novel is the experience only of paradise lost.

In presenting Anthony Patch's experience in *The Beautiful and Damned*, Fitzgerald achieves a greater sense of unity and coherence than he had done in *This Side of Paradise*. As we have already seen, he recognized that the writing mode employed in the second novel was quite unlike that of the first. *The Beautiful and Damned* is longer, fuller, more comprehensive; the social world inhabited by Anthony and Gloria is portrayed in much more detail. Likewise, to use Fitzgerald's own terms, the novel is more 'psychological' than 'dramatic'. What this means is that the inner lives and emotions of the principal characters, Anthony and Gloria, are rendered with the same fullness as the external social world. Lastly, despite the use of headings, as in the first novel, and the occasional reversal to passages of dramatic dialogue and other expressionistic devices, the basic mode of *The Beautiful and Damned* is that of a straightforward realism. The result is an overall advance on *The Side of Paradise* in terms of structural unity, characterization, and consistency of tone.

The opening of the novel reveals a new confidence, a sureness of touch that has nothing immature about it. Here, for example, is a description of Anthony Patch's elderly grandfather, fabulously wealthy but obsessed with a campaign for national moral reform:

> The span of his seventy-five years had acted as a magic bellows – the first quarter-century had blown him full with life, and the last had sucked it all back. It had sucked in the cheeks and the chest and the girth of arm and leg. It had tyrannously demanded his teeth, one by one, suspended his small eyes in dark-bluish sacks, tweeked out his hairs, changed him from grey to white in some places, from pink to yellow in others – callously transposing his colours like a child trying over a paintbox. Then through his body and his soul it had attacked his brain. It had sent him night-sweats and tears and unfounded dreads. It had split his intense normality into credulity and suspicion. Out of the

[6]John Coyle makes a similar point in his comparative study of *Gatsby* and Alain Fournier's *Le Grand Meaulnes:* 'Meaulnes and Gatsby' in *Essays in Poetics*, 12 (1987), pp. 15–40.

coarse material of his enthusiasm it had cut dozens of meek but petulant obsessions; his energy was shrunk to the bad temper of a spoiled child, and for his will to power was substituted a fatuous puerile desire for a land of harps and canticles on earth.[7]

The vivid economy of this Fitzgerald perhaps owes to his work in the short-story form, but the result is that there is nothing more we need to learn about Adam Patch: his behaviour in the rest of the novel simply amounts to an acting-out of what we have here. A passage from much later in the novel is equally efficient at evoking a specific emotional condition. Anthony and Gloria are leaving their house in the Connecticut countryside and returning, defeated, to New York:

> Came a day in September, a day slashed with alternate sun and rain, sun without warmth, rain without freshness. On that day they left the grey house, which had seen the flower of their love. Four trunks and three monstrous crates were piled in the dismantled room where, two years before, they had sprawled lazily, thinking in terms of dreams, remote, languorous, content. The room echoed with emptiness. Gloria, in a new brown dress edged with fur, sat upon a trunk in silence, and Anthony walked nervously to and fro smoking, as they waited for the truck that would take their things to the city.   (p. 230)

Every element, every detail of this description, works to suggest the bitter deterioration in the relationship between the two. Each item of physical description is edged with emotion. The sense of loss, of frustration and failure is total. Whole sections of this novel are written with just this degree of assured control. Of course *The Beautiful and Damned* sometimes reverts, as Zelda noted, to a kind of literary and intellectual pretentiousness, when Fitzgerald tries to prove he is as bright as his critical friends, but these passages do not undermine the achieved power of the novel as a whole.

II

More than most authors, Fitzgerald drew upon the experience of his own life as source material for his fiction. From the successful publication of *This Side of Paradise* onwards, financial necessity drove him to produce a constant stream of short stories for the high paying

[7]F. Scott Fitzgerald, *The Beautiful and Damned* (Penguin Books, 1966), p. 18. All subsequent references are to this edition.

American magazine market. Perhaps it was this need that made him convert almost everything that he did, everything that happened to him, into fictional material. In this context it is hardly surprising that today's readers of *The Beautiful and Damned*, with its central focus on the slow and painful cracking-up of the marriage between the privileged Anthony and the beautiful Gloria, assume that the novel is largely about Fitzgerald and Zelda. In a sense of course they are right. Fitzgerald himself was in no doubt about the relevance of the novel to his own life with Zelda. In 1930 he wrote to his wife:

> I wish the Beautiful and Damned had been a maturely written book because it was all true. We ruined ourselves – I have never honestly thought that we ruined each other.[8]

Ten years later, writing to his daughter, he seems to qualify the autobiographical dimension of the book, but does not repudiate it:

> Gloria was a much more trivial and vulgar person than your mother. I can't really say there was any resemblance except in the beauty and certain terms of expression she used, and also I naturally used many circumstantial events of our early married life. However the emphases were entirely different. We had a much better time than Anthony and Gloria had.[9]

There is then a close connection between Anthony and Gloria and Fitzgerald and Zelda. But we need to be careful here. *The Beautiful and Damned* was published in 1922; the Fitzgeralds' marriage was in 1920. The novel charts the slow disintegration of a marriage over a long period of years. In 1922 no one would have predicted that the bright young Fitzgeralds were trapped in a marriage that would end in alcoholism and madness. The benefit of hindsight allows us to identify the source of the sense of pain and bitterness in the novel in Fitzgerald's own life with Zelda; but this was far from obvious at the time. And hindsight is in danger of distorting the novel, if we read into it a history that was still, at the time of writing, very much in the future.

For the great majority of readers and critics in 1922, Fitzgerald and Zelda were nothing more than famously beautiful people. And this is why *The Beautiful and Damned* surprised – and perhaps disappointed – the contemporary reading-public. On the basis of *This Side of Paradise*, and the early collection of short stories *Flappers*

---

[8]See Bruccoli, *Some Sort of Epic Grandeur*, p. 155.
[9]Bruccoli, *Op. cit*, p. 155.

and Philosophers (1920), it had been assumed that Fitzgerald's only subject was the rich and the glamorous. And there was already a question over how far the author was taken in by the superficial charm of the world his stories evoked so brilliantly: did he recognize the moral corruption of the Jazz Age society he continually wrote about? But here was *The Beautiful and Damned*, a long novel portraying not the glitter and glamour of the lives of the young, the beautiful and privileged, but rather the slow, irresistible draining away of youthful charm and hope into bleakness and despair. Clearly something has gone wrong – this is not Fitzgerald's kind of book.

The explanation for the change offered by critics at the time was one which incidentally reflected the view that Fitzgerald was a witless writer with no artistic or aesthetic principles of his own. The bleaker tone of *The Beautiful and Damned* derives from the works of the American literary naturalists whom Fitzgerald had been reading: he is simply repeating the disillusioned, pessimistic view of life and its meaning – or non-meaning – he has found in Dreiser, Frank Norris, Harold Frederic and the rest. This is the view put forward, for example, in Edmund Wilson's *Bookman* article. Fitzgerald in other words is a kind of sponge, soaking up and regurgitating whatever modish literary fashion happens to come his way; he is not a conscious artist in his own right. The point is not that Fitzgerald's portrayal of Anthony Patch's slow decline owes nothing at all to literary sources. In fact there is a clear debt to Dreiser's *Sister Carrie* and Norris's *Vandover and the Brute*. But it is absurd to see the whole portrayal of the lives of Anthony and Gloria, from the early brilliance to the despairing end, as no more than an extended pastiche of American literary naturalism. Robert Roulston's more recent conclusion is altogether more convincing:

> . . . surely the bitterness, the unrelenting misogyny, the want of *joie de vivre*, and the almost equal contempt for those who strive and those who repine owe more to Fitzgerald's own state of mind than to literary or philosophical models.[10]

The Beautiful and Damned has obvious links with Fitzgerald's last completed novel, *Tender is the Night*. Both works are concerned to present a similar movement from early promise to eventual failure and defeat. Perhaps then it is not surprising that both novels have been subjected to the same basic criticism: that Fitzgerald fails to clarify

[10]Robert Roulston, 'The Beautiful and Damned: The Alcoholic's Revenge,' *Literature and Pyschology*, 27 (1977), p. 162.

the causes of the decline that overtakes his protagonists – a point of view that seems to assume that the explanation of failure is more important than the experience of it. At the opening of the novel, the promises of life all seem to be within Anthony Patch's grasp. A recent Harvard graduate, he is intelligent, sensitive, sophisticated. He is his multi-millionaire grandfather's sole heir. He is in a position to make of his life whatever he chooses. What in fact he chooses is marriage to Gloria Gilbert, a beauty from the Middle West, who has much in common with Rosalind in *This Side of Paradise*. Like Rosalind, Gloria is preoccupied above all with herself, with for example her legs, and the need to acquire a suntan. Anthony learns that 'Well, this girl talked about legs. She talked about skin too – her own skin. Always her own. She told me the sort of tan she'd like to get in the summer and how closely she usually approximated it.' (p. 45) If Gloria looks back to Rosalind in *This Side of Paradise* she also looks forward to Nicole in *Tender is the Night*. For both women, the world exists to service them: in a famous passage in Chapter Twelve of *Tender is the Night* Nicole Diver is described as 'the product of much ingenuity and toil' – all the wheels of America's industrial capitalism turn to produce the wealth she spends so lavishly on presents in Paris, but already in *The Beautiful and Damned* Gloria 'took all the things of life for hers to choose from and apportion, as though she were continually picking out presents for herself from an inexhaustible counter.' (p. 55) Gloria's emphatic selfishness, and Anthony's inability to decide on a career he can undertake – his grandfather constantly presses him on the point – are no doubt meant to signal future problems, but it is true that Fitzgerald offers no single explanation of the decline that begins almost as soon as the marriage ceremony is over. A variety of factors, some of them perhaps contradictory, seem to be involved.

Much of the time Fitzgerald portrays Anthony as temperamentally weak and morally irresponsible. He knows very well he should settle down and do something, earn his living. Early on he tells himself that 'If I am essentially weak . . . I need work to do, work to do.' (p. 49) But his attempts at work are never more than half-hearted; discouraged, he simply gives up. It is so much simpler to throw another party, have a drink at the Ritz, invite some friends around . . . Work can be postponed until another time. Yet the novel also suggests that Anthony's slide into disintegration and defeat is not solely a question of his own lack of resolution and moral weakness. The world he is living in is one corrupted by money and its own cynicism. In 1938 Fitzgerald suggested to his daughter that 'his generation of radicals and breakers-down never found anything to take the place of the old virtues of work and courage and the old graces of courtesy and politeness.'[11] Anthony Patch makes a similar discovery. Despite the fact that the life he leads with Gloria epitomizes Jazz Age recklessness – as though the party can go on forever – there is something old-fashioned about Anthony, a kind of diffidence that makes him subtly unfitted to succeed in the society of which he is part. Then there is the problem of Gloria: is it Anthony's addiction to her, rather than to alcohol, that is the source of his problems? Anthony himself finally believes that 'all the distress that he had ever known, the sorrow and the pain, had been because of women.' (p. 360) Fitzgerald may not wholly endorse this view, but Gloria clearly has all the negative characteristics of the glamorous but irresponsible woman who recurs throughout Fitzgerald's fiction: she had wanted nothing, we are told, 'except to be young and beautiful for a long time, to be gay and happy, and to have money and love.' (p. 226) Anthony's marriage to Gloria, for all its initial glamour, is certainly portrayed as a major factor in his decline. Or is it the case that the novel is suggesting that decline is built into the nature of things – is life no more than a process of gradual running down or wearing away? Sometimes it appears that such a view – which he could have found in the American literary naturalists – does appeal to Fitzgerald.

The point is that Fitzgerald may well not have known how precisely and consistently to explain the failure he was portraying. But what he could do was imagine its movement, its successive stages, with such impressive power that a comparison with Dreiser's portrayal of the fall of Hurstwood in *Sister Carrie* is in no way inappropriate. Particularly from the brilliant theatrical moment when Anthony's puritanical grandfather arrives in the midst of the novel's wildest party in Marietta, to its bleak ending, the novel offers a series of episodes and scenes which dramatize Anthony's personal decline, and the disintegration of his marriage, with compelling conviction. The vivid and evocative account of the South, and Anthony's involvement with Dorothy Raycroft during his army training; his attempt at becoming a salesman in New York; his drinking at Sammy's; the drunken and violent confrontation with Bloeckman – all of these scenes are effectively and dramatically portrayed. It may be true that when Anthony and Gloria and their friends discuss life and its meaning – or lack of meaning – then the pace and tension in *The Beautiful and Damned* are inclined to flag. On the other hand, when what is being scrutinized and analysed is not 'life' in general, but the

[11]Turnbull, *Op. cit*, p. 51.

particulars of the relationship between Anthony and Gloria, then the case is very difficult. Every detail seems to count, and pretentiousness is replaced by a hard honesty and authenticity that make the analysis wholly convincing. Immaturity is precisely what is not present here.

III

In Fitzgerald's letter to Edmund Wilson about the *Bookman* article, he insisted that he had intended Anthony and Gloria to be representative figures: 'They are two of the great army of the rootless who float around New York. There must be thousands.' He concedes, however, that he 'didn't bring it out.'[12] The comment is nonetheless of interest as it suggests a specific way of approaching and reading the novel. Seen thus, *The Beautiful and Damned* is a novel of manners or social comment; what it does, is expose the careless and useless lives of the essentially hollow people who compose Jazz Age 1920s society; what it reveals is the dark reality that lies beneath the superficial glamour and charm. In fact this is a quite plausible reading. *The Beautiful and Damned* is in one sense Fitzgerald's 'Waste Land' novel, evoking the sterility, hopelessness, and loss of values of the postwar modern world. In an essay called 'Early Success,' written in 1937, Fitzgerald describes how, in the period after the success of *This Side of Paradise*, he had developed a sense of the undercurrent of violence and danger in the booming America of the early 20s: 'All the stories that came into my head had a touch of disaster in them – the lovely young creatures in my novels went to ruin, the diamond mountains of my short stories blew up, my millionaires were as beautiful and damned as Thomas Hardy's peasants.' And he goes on to say that he was 'pretty sure living wasn't the reckless, careless business these people thought – this generation just younger than me.'[13] *The Beautiful and Damned* gives considerable substance to these comments; its text and subtext articulate a general sense of a society lacking direction or purpose, morally confused, potentially violent. Yet the actual violence portrayed in the novel is personal in its nature: Anthony and Gloria fighting horrifically on the railway platform until Anthony is left with blood spurting from his thumb; Anthony's futile drunken attack on Bloeckman in which he is left lying on the ground, his mouth full of blood; or Anthony's mad,

---

[12]Turnbull, *Op. cit*, pp. 351–52.
[13]'Early Success' in the *Crack-Up with other Pieces and Stories* (Penguin Books, 1965), pp. 59–60.

hysterical attack on Dorothy Raycroft – 'I'll kill you,' 'I'll kill you' – he shouts, near the end of the novel. As always in Fitzgerald, the wider implications spiral outward from the carefully observed personal level; the individual context dominates, and the consciousness that is responding to and recording experience remains that of Fitzgerald himself. Thus the dimension of *The Beautiful and Damned* that makes it a novel of manners is not readily isolated from the novel's focus on the individual life, while the individual concerns that arise in the novel inevitably include those that preoccupy the author himself.

In 1920, writing about the new novel he was then at work on (provisionally entitled *The Flight of the Rocket*), Fitzgerald said of his protagonist Anthony Patch: 'He is one of those many with the tastes and weaknesses of an artist but with no actual creative inspiration.'[14] From the first, that is, Fitzgerald had conceived of Anthony as a version of the inadequate or failed artist; and in the course of the novel Anthony does make several attempts to rescue his position by becoming a writer. But the Amory Blaine who ends *This Side of Paradise,* not yet ready to put pen to paper, though 'preserved to help in building up the living consciousness of the race' will find no kind of Joycean fulfilment in the ineffectual efforts of Anthony Patch. At first Anthony believes he can become a kind of gentlemanly historian writing a history of the Middle Ages or the Renaissance popes; he even gets as far as completing an introductory essay on the twelfth century. Later, when his financial needs are becoming ever more pressing, he tries to raise some cash by producing short stories for the popular magazine market. But the six stories, 'by a man who had never before made a consistent effort to write at all,' (p. 248) are a dismal failure. For most of the novel, Anthony's writing exists only as an unrealizable ambition – it is something he can tell his grandfather, and Gloria, that he is about to do. Anthony knows that his pleasure-seeking way of life with Gloria is subtly atrophying whatever intellectual capacities he may once have had; he knows too that his grandfather believes he intended to do nothing at all. But even so his attempt at writing is never wholly serious: at best it is a painful gesture. In a crucial scene, Gloria attacks him for promising much, for going through the motions, but achieving nothing:

[14]Turnbull, *Op. cit,* p. 163.

'Work!' she scoffed. 'Oh, you sad bird! You bluffer! Work – that
means a great arranging of the desk and the lights, a great sharpening
of pencils, and "Gloria, don't sing!" and "Please keep that damn Tana
away from me", and "Let me read you my opening sentence", and "I
won't be through for a long time, Gloria, so don't stay up for me", and
a tremendous consumption of tea or coffee. And that's all. In just about
an hour I hear the old pencil stop scratching and look over. You've got
out a book and you're "looking up" something. Then you're reading.
Then yawns – then bed and a great tossing about because you're all
full of caffeine and can't sleep. Two weeks later the whole performance
over again.'   (pp. 175–76)

The scorn and derision present here are more than enough to discom-
fit Anthony; he can find little to say in reply. Inevitably, however,
one is persuaded that the power of the scene derives from its source
in Fitzgerald's own experience – just as elsewhere in *The Beautiful
and Damned* he gives expression to other aspects of the problems
and tensions he was experiencing as man and writer. Through the
character of Richard Caramel, for example, Fitzgerald articulates a
fear about his own future as a writer that was already beginning to
haunt him. Caramel surprises his friends by publishing a novel that
is both successful and good; in his subsequent work, however, artistic
integrity is sacrificed to financial considerations. After the success
of *This Side of Paradise* Fitzgerald himself came to believe that
the constant need to produce commercially acceptable material for
The Saturday Evening Post and other magazines was preventing him
from writing serious novels. Eventually he would regard his magazine
stories as a way of buying time to allow him to work on his serious
fiction. But it is through the picture of Anthony Patch – the man and
the would-be writer – that Fitzgerald gives fullest expression to his
own increasing doubts and uncertainties.

Anthony Patch is endowed with beauty, charm and wealth: for him
all the promise that life has to offer seems to be eminently attainable.
Gloria becomes the glittering symbol of the paradise he is seeking;
and with his marriage he appears to have taken possession. But just
as Gatsby discovers, after his reunion with Daisy, that the famous
green light at the end of the dock ceases to be an enchanted object,
so Anthony discovers that Gloria's reality belongs not to paradise but
to a flawed and fallen world. Anthony's problem is that he is both
committed to that world and repelled by it. The situation he is in is
suggested in an almost emblematic manner in a crucial scene which
occurs on the night before his marriage. Anthony lies in bed thinking
that Gloria's reality, her physical existence, and the union of his soul

with hers, carries him into a plane beyond anything he has experienced in the books he has read: her 'radiant fire and freshness was the living material of which the dead beauty of books was made.' (p. 125) As he ponders, he becomes aware of a confirmatory sound in the city around him:

> From the night into his high-walled room there came, persistently, that evanescent and dissolving sound – something the city was tossing up and calling back again, like a child playing with a ball. In Harlem, the Bronx, Gramercy Park, and along the water-fronts, in little parlours or on pebble-strewn, moon-flooded roofs, a thousand lovers were making this sound, crying little fragments of it into the air. All the city was playing with this sound out there in the blue summer dark, throwing it up and calling it back, promising that, in a little while, life would be beautiful as a story, promising happiness – and by that promise giving it. (p. 125)

But this lyrical, romantic promise of life and love is suddenly shattered. Anthony hears a different, more raucous sound. A woman is laughing nearby, loudly, hysterically; a man's voice is also just discernible. Anthony finds the sound 'at first amazing, then strangely terrible.' The woman's voice rises to a scream – then breaks off. Anthony is menaced by the ensuing silence. His earlier feelings of romantic hopes and dreams are utterly destroyed. Life has struck back with a kind of coarse violence:

> [Anthony] found himself upset and shaken. Try as he might to strangle his reaction, some animal quality in that unrestrained laughter had grasped at his imagination, and for the first time in four months aroused his old aversion and horror toward all the business of life. The room had grown smothery. He wanted to be out in some cool and bitter breeze, miles above the cities, and to live serene and detached back in the corners of his mind. Life was that sound out there, that ghastly reiterated female sound. (p. 126)

Anthony's impulse here to retreat, to withdraw from a reality that is too harsh to be endurable is linked to the subsequent revelation that he is an exceptionally fearful, even cowardly, young man. Fitzgerald clearly expects the reader to regard this as evidence of Anthony's essential weakness, his lack of moral strength of any kind. But in the passage just quoted, the alternative that Anthony longs for is instructive: 'to live serene and detached back in the corners of his mind.' Serenity and detachment suggest the observer of life rather than the participant in it. Anthony we know is a figure of the artist manqué. What the passage does is dramatize in extreme terms the choice between art and life. Once married to Gloria, Anthony is committed to life. And for them both what life means is a more and more frantic pursuit of instant happiness and pleasure. The vague philosophical notions that Anthony debates with his friends offer him no firm, alternative resource. As time passes both Anthony and Gloria lose control of their lives: they are used up by the life they have chosen, a life in which the ugliness of a woman's scream does indeed shatter romantic dreams of love and happiness. For Anthony Patch the serenity and detachment of art prove out of reach; life destroys even the possibility of art. By 1922 Fitzgerald was already alert to the possibility that his life could prove destructive of his art. That is the fear that provides the subtext of *The Beautiful and Damned*.

The *Beautiful and Damned* appeared in the *Publishers Weekly* monthly bestsellers' list for March, April and May, 1922 – *This Side of Paradise* had made the same list only twice. The initial sales of the two novels were very much the same: around fifty thousand copies. But *The Beautiful and Damned* did little to advance Fitzgerald's contemporary reputation. H.L. Mencken and Henry Seidel Canby praised the novel, but the lengthy commentaries by Fitzgerald's Princeton friends, John Peale Bishop and Edmund Wilson, as we have seen mingling praise with patronizing criticism, did much to establish the disparaging critical orthodoxy which Fitzgerald, and his early novels in particular, have suffered from ever since. To go behind that tradition is not to discover lost masterpieces. It is to discover two eminently readable novels which significantly illuminate Fitzgerald's career as a writer.

4

The Great Gatsby

I

When Fitzgerald began writing the novel that was to become *The Great Gatsby* early in 1924, he was aware that his literary career had made little progress since the appearance of *The Beautiful and Damned* two years earlier. Writing to Maxwell Perkins around April, 1924, he acknowledged that it was 'only in the last four months that I've realized how much I've, well, almost *deteriorated* in the three years since I finished *The Beautiful and Damned*.' Now he is determined to change all that utilizing the 'enormous power' he feels he possesses. The new book may take some time to write but it will involve 'the sustained imagination of a sincere yet radiant world' and it 'will be a consciously artistic achievement and must depend on that as the first books did not.'[1] Even earlier, in the spring of 1922, he had written to Perkins that he wanted 'to write something *new* – something extraordinary and beautiful and simple and intricately patterned.'[2] The aesthetic ambitiousness involved in the composition of *The Great Gatsby* had been sparked in part by Fitzgerald's reading of Conrad. In his 1934 Introduction to the Modern Library edition of *Gatsby*, Fitzgerald tells us that in approaching the writing of *Gatsby* he 'had just re-read Joseph Conrad's Preface to *The Nigger [of the Narcissus]*' – which is an articulation of Conrad's own aesthetic credo as a novelist. Fitzgerald clearly found Conrad's beliefs deeply sympathetic, and it is not too

[1] Andrew Turnbull, ed., *The Letters of F. Scott Fitzgerald* (Penguin Books, 1968) pp. 181–82.
[2] See Bruccoli, *Some Sort of Epic Grandeur*, p. 170.

difficult to see why this should be so. Conrad offered Fitzgerald just the kind of sustenance and support that his critics had been denying him. Conrad's Preface made it clear to Fitzgerald that his power as an artist had nothing to do with how brilliant a mind he had, how deep a thinker he was. For Conrad the artist is not like the thinker or scientist; the sources of aesthetic power lie deep within the individual self; the appeal of the artist is not to our wisdom or ideas, but to our enduring 'capacity for delight and wonder, to the sense of mystery surrounding our lives; to our sense of pity, and beauty, and pain . . .' For Conrad, 'All art . . . appeals primarily to the senses, and the artistic aim when expressing itself in written words must also make its appeal through the senses, if its high desire is to reach the secret spring of responsive emotions.' Thus the writer must aim at 'the perfect blending of form and substance,' must show 'an unremitting never-discouraged care for the shape and ring of sentences' and allow 'the light of magic suggestiveness' to 'play for an evanescent instant over the commonplace surface of words.' Conrad's famous conclusion is that as an artist his task is 'by the power of the written word to make you hear, to make you feel – it is, before all, to make you see.' Only thus does art communicate truth. For Fitzgerald, so long badgered by critics complaining of his lack of intellectual sophistication, of his naiveté and immaturity, particularly in relation to ideas, all of this must have seemed like manna from a critical heaven. Conrad was offering crucial endorsement of what Fitzgerald as an artist was particularly equipped to do: 'delight and wonder,' 'pity, and beauty, and pain' – were not these precisely the mainsprings of his art? Writing *The Great Gatsby* he would simply go ahead, building on his strengths, and aiming above all to produce a finished work of art that would, just as Conrad required, 'carry its justification in every line.'

As the writing of *Gatsby* progressed in 1924 Fitzgerald grew increasingly confident of its quality. In August he told Maxwell Perkins – more or less seriously – that it was 'about the best American novel ever written.'[3] In October, when the manuscript was complete, he told Perkins. 'I think that at last I've done something really my own. . . .'[4] Before the novel was published he told another correspondent: 'My new novel appears in late March: *The Great Gatsby*. It represents about a year's work and I think it's about

[3]Turnbull, *Op. cit*, p. 185.
[4]Turnbull, *Op. cit*, p. 186.

ten years better than anything I've done.'[5] Despite such bravado and show of self-belief; despite the new seriousness of intent with which he had approached the writing of *Gatsby*; and despite the degree of reassurance he received from his reading of Conrad's Preface to *The Nigger of the Narcissus*, Fitzgerald was too much himself not to suffer moments of doubt and loss of confidence in what he had written right up to the time of publication in April, 1925. At every stage in the publication process he revised, rewrote, altered, shifted material around. And most of these changes did represent improvements. One aspect of the novel which he was never happy about, however, was its title. At different times he considered a variety of titles: *Trimalchio* (after the party-giver in Petronius's *Satyricon*), *Trimalchio in West Egg*, *Among Ash-Heaps and Millionaires*, *On the Road to West Egg*, *Gold-Hatted Gatsby*, *The High-Bouncing Lover*. Zelda and Perkins both preferred *The Great Gatsby* and in the end he settled for that, but without much enthusiasm. Later, when the sales of the novel failed to live up to his expectations, he argued that the title was partially responsible. More interesting is his explanation to Perkins of why he disliked the title: '*The Great Gatsby* is weak because there's no emphasis even ironically on his greatness or lack of it.'[6] The denial of ironic intent here has to be attended to: it hardly supports the view that we are to see Gatsby as a kind of hollow man, the sham creation of wild rumour and speculation. On the other hand some readers at least will be reluctant to agree with Fitzgerald that there is absolutely nothing great about Gatsby.

When *The Great Gatsby* appeared Fitzgerald responded to criticism in ways that suggest, as we shall see, that he did not always recognize just how successful he had been in 'making us *see*' in the novel. As usual, he was much too ready to go along with his critics. Nonetheless he did know that with *Gatsby* he had lifted himself to a new level of achievement. When he told Perkins that he could again believe he was 'a wonderful writer' and that he was 'much better than any of the young Americans *without exception*,'[7] he had reached a position of belief in himself as an artist that was for him entirely new. The question was, having reached that position, could he remain there? The answer was, of course, that he could not; in this, as in so many aspects of Fitzgerald's life and career, such self-confidence would

[5]Turnbull, *Op. cit*, p. 498.
[6]Turnbull, *Op. cit*, p. 196.
[7]Turnbull, *Op. cit*, pp. 192–8.

prove only temporary.

Published in April, 1925, *The Great Gatsby* simultaneously fulfilled and dashed Fitzgerald's greatest hopes. The major disappointment was over sales: compared with both *This Side of Paradise* and *The Beautiful and Damned, The Great Gatsby* was, inexplicably, a failure: initial sales slowly crept over twenty thousand, but Fitzgerald had been confidently expecting three or four times as many. He came up with different explanations: the title was wrong, as he had suspected all along; more importantly, the book contained no important woman character 'and women control the fiction market at present;'[8] later he decided that spring publication had been a bad idea – the fall would have been better. Whatever the reason, the sales of *Gatsby* refused to pick up, and Fitzgerald knew perfectly clearly what this meant: back to the writing of short fiction for the commercial market in the hope of creating enough financial space to write another novel. If this proves impossibly difficult, he talks for the first time of giving up as a novelist and going to Hollywood to 'learn the movie business.'[9]

Yet *Gatsby*, a failure as a bestseller, brought Fitzgerald one immense consolation prize: the critical acclaim as a serious writer he had always longed for. As it happened, the early reviews of the novel were somewhat disappointing. Fitzgerald wrote to Perkins: 'I think all the reviews I've seen, except two, have been absolutely stupid and lousy. Someday they'll eat grass, by God!'[10] (On this point at least Fitzgerald was right.) What had happened, he decided, was that the reviewers had not understood *Gatsby* and so had been reluctant to commit themselves either way: 'Most of the reviewers' he wrote, 'floundered around in a piece of work that obviously they completely failed to understand and tried to give it reviews that committed them neither pro or con until someone of culture had spoken.'[11] Even when better reviews did begin to appear, Fitzgerald remained convinced that his book was not being understood. To Edmund Wilson he wrote: '. . . of all the reviews, even the most enthusiastic, not one had the slightest idea what the book was about. . . .'[12] What did delight Fitzgerald, however, was the almost universal chorus of praise that *Gatsby* received from all those figures in the literary world whom he admired and respected: Wilson himself of course, H.L. Mencken, Edith Wharton, James Branch Cabell, Gertrude Stein in Paris, the

[8]Turnbull, *Op. cit*, p. 199.
[9]Turnbull, *Op. cit*, p. 199.
[10]Turnbull, *Op. cit*, p. 198.
[11]Turnbull, *Op. cit*, p. 200.
[12]Turnbull, *Op. cit*, p. 362.

new young American writer whom Fitzgerald was encouraging, also in Paris – Ernest Hemingway. And perhaps most prized of all, a letter from T.S. Eliot telling Fitzgerald he had read *Gatsby* three times and considered it 'the first step forward American fiction had taken since Henry James.' *The Great Gatsby* failed to make Fitzgerald the money he needed; it did, however, make his critical name.

II

The key to *The Great Gatsby*'s success as a novel – and the reason why it does represent a major advance in Fitzgerald's art of fiction – lies in its form, and its narrative form in particular. Both *This Side of Paradise* and *The Beautiful and Damned* suffer from Fitzgerald's uneven control of narrative structure. Both early novels are told from the point of view of an intermittently omniscient author – but the degree of intervention by the author varies in a quite arbitrary manner. Equally both novels contain sections in which narrative is temporarily replaced by dramatization – as though we are suddenly reading the script of a play. The consistent use of Nick Carraway as an internal narrator imposes a new kind of narrative discipline on *The Great Gatsby*: the result is a satisfying sense of formal unity and coherence. Fitzgerald told H.L. Mencken that he had patterned *Gatsby* 'in protest against my own formless two novels.' But as always, here too he was capable of underestimating his own success.

Despite all the praise it received, Fitzgerald was convinced that *Gatsby* contained one major flaw. This is how he described it to Edmund Wilson:

> The worst fault in it [the book's design], I think is a BIG FAULT: I gave no account (and had no feeling about or knowledge of) the emotional relations between Gatsby and Daisy from the time of their reunion to the catastrophe. However, the lack is so astutely concealed by the retrospect of Gatsby's past and by blankets of excellent prose that no one has noticed it – tho everyone has felt the lack and called it by another name.[13]

Fitzgerald repeated the point to Mencken in almost identical terms:

---

[13]Turnbull, *Op. cit*, pp. 361–62.

There is a tremendous fault in the book – the lack of an emotional presentment of Daisy's attitude towards Gatsby after their reunion (and the consequent lack of logic or importance in her throwing him over). Everyone has felt this but no one has spotted it because it's concealed beneath elaborate and overlapping blankets of prose.[14]

But on this crucial point it is clear that Fitzgerald wrote better than he knew: Lawrence's dictum that we should trust the tale and not the teller applies. What Fitzgerald is describing here as a weakness is in fact a strength. What he is blaming himself for having failed to provide – a fuller account of the emotional relationship between Gatsby and Daisy and particularly of Daisy's feelings towards Gatsby – is precisely what we have no way of knowing, and indeed precisely what we are a great deal better off *not* knowing.

In making the remarks about the Daisy–Gatsby emotional relationship, Fitzgerald is forgetting the kind of novel he has written, and the particular narrative form he has chosen to use. He is forgetting that he has written what he will later call a 'dramatic' novel rather than a psychological one. He is speaking of Gatsby and Daisy as though they were characters in *The Beautiful and Damned*, to be presented with the same fullness of psychological detail as Anthony and Gloria. But this is simply not the case. With Nicole and Dick Diver in *Tender is the Night* Fitzgerald will return to the fullness of treatment, the psychological and emotional comprehensiveness, the weight of detail, of his second novel. But in *Gatsby* the method is more selective: psychological realism is not what is striven for. In fact realism itself is highly selective, coexisting with other more poetic and expressionistic modes. What the characters mean, what they represent, is more important than what they are. As a character Gatsby of course can have no consciousness of his own significance – what his life really means – which is why Nick Carraway's role, and the narrative method Fitzgerald has chosen, are of such crucial importance.

Nick Carraway controls the storytelling of *The Great Gatsby* from beginning to end. He is looking back on recent events in his own life, telling us the story of his involvement with Gatsby, the Buchanans, Jordan Baker and the rest of the characters. Given that he is a character in the story, as well as narrator of it, he of course can have no privileged access to the interior emotional lives of the other characters. He can tell us only what they tell him, or what he learns, deduces or thinks for himself. Thus, without abandoning the narrative

[14]Turnbull, *Op. cit*, p. 499.

procedure he had chosen, there was no way in which Fitzgerald could have allowed us direct entry into the emotional lives and responses of Daisy and Gatsby. The emotional relations between Gatsby and Daisy, despite what Fitzgerald says in his letters, are as present as they can be – given the limits of what Nick Carraway can possibly know.

Would the novel have benefited from an alternative narrative procedure? It is difficult to believe that it would. Carraway's narrative role seems absolutely crucial to the novel's success. The decision to delegate the storytelling to a character-narrator like Carraway, Fitzgerald almost certainly owed to his reading of Conrad. As we have already seen, he was an admirer of Conrad who had regularly made use of a narrator figure in his novels and stories. Henry James, whom Fitzgerald also admired, was another novelist who had seen and exploited the potential of the character-narrator figure. All the critical and aesthetic advantages which his famous predecessors had found and developed in the use of character-narrators were thus available to Fitzgerald: greater reader involvement, an increased sense of immediacy, and a much intensified illusion of reality (I was there, all this happened to me). But, whether consciously or not, the decision to allow Nick Carraway to tell the story of Gatsby, gave Fitzgerald a way of ordering and controlling his own involvement with the material that had not been present in his earlier novels. Unusually, what is involved is a move towards not greater complexity of character but rather greater simplicity. Amory Blaine and Anthony Patch are divided, even self-contradictory, protagonists. Amory longs for success while simultaneously disapproving of it; Anthony Patch pursues life as a kind of romantic daydream, while at the same time upbraiding himself over his failure to get down to work. The author's own attitude towards both characters is unclear; he seems caught up in the emotional contradictions. What happens in *Gatsby* is that Fitzgerald splits off his own complex feelings about his life, his simultaneous sense of involvement and detachment, into two separate characters: Nick Carraway absorbs Fitzgerald's feelings of responsibility, moral objectivity, and a kind of artistic detachment, while Fitzgerald's romanticism, his total involvement with life and commitment to it, go into the creation of Jay Gatsby.

Yet the distinction between Nick and Gatsby is never absolute, and both characters are allowed sufficient complexity of feeling to make them exist as fully individual human beings. In certain moods, at certain times, Nick Carraway, aware of his exclusion from the vibrant life going on around him, regrets exactly his detachment, his isolated role:

> At the enchanted metropolitan twilight I felt a haunting loneliness sometimes, and felt it in others – poor young clerks who loitered in front of windows waiting until it was time for a solitary restaurant dinner – young clerks in the dusk, wasting the most poignant moments of night and life.
>
> Again at eight o'clock, when the dark lanes of the Forties were five deep with throbbing taxicabs, bound for the theatre district, I felt a sinking in my heart. Forms leaned together in the taxis as they waited, and voices sang, and there was laughter from unheard jokes, and lighted cigarettes outlined unintelligible gestures inside. Imagining that I, too, was hurrying toward gayety and sharing their intimate excitement, I wished them well.[15]

Fitzgerald's artist figures regularly worry over the possibility of missing out on life. As artist-narrator, Nick Carraway can only function by remaining the detached observer of the events in which he is involved, but the passage reveals Fitzgerald's sensitive awareness of what the cost of detachment may be. Similarly, Gatsby's commitment to life is far from unqualified. His commitment to Daisy is absolute, but, as we shall see, his apparent detachment from most of the life around him is one of his most striking characteristics. Despite these qualifications, however, the creation of the two characters has afforded Fitzgerald a new degree of artistic control over his own emotional complicity with the materials out of which *The Great Gatsby* is created: involvement and detachment co-exist in the text, and the contradictions and confusions of the earlier novels disappear.

If it is difficult to see how a different narrative procedure would have benefited *The Great Gatsby*, it is even more difficult to see how more material about the emotional reactions of Daisy and Gatsby towards each other would have improved the text. Whatever Fitzgerald may have believed, the fact that Nick Carraway keeps us at arm's length from the inner consciousness of Daisy and Gatsby is much more of a strength than a weakness. It is difficult to believe that further insight into their awareness would supply us with anything except more of the 'appalling sentimentality' (p. 118) which Nick recognizes in Gatsby's account of how he fell in love with Daisy. The more detail we had about Gatsby's feelings for Daisy the more difficult it would be to

---

[15]F. Scott Fitzgerald, *The Great Gatsby* (Penguin Books, 1950), pp. 63–64. All subsequent references are to this edition.

avoid a devaluing of all his visionary dreaming and romantic yearning; his romanticism and idealism would appear too flawed to be taken seriously. As it is, the reader does recognize the immense irony of Gatsby's having embodied all his hopes and dreams in a vessel as fragile as Daisy Buchanan. Having made us above all 'see' this, Fitzgerald-Carraway has accomplished one of his major tasks. Further details of Gatsby's inner life – his thoughts and feelings about Daisy – are not required. Their essential character is clear enough, and they are not what makes Gatsby interesting to us. Gatsby has an interest that is not merely personal; it is what he represents that matters, not what in detail he is like. Nick Carraway's job as narrator is to make us see Gatsby as he comes to see him. Greater detail about Daisy and Gatsby's feelings towards each other would not have improved the novel. Rather it would have blurred the picture that Nick Carraway attempts to paint.

III

This Side of Paradise and *The Beautiful and Damned* have been neglected by critics and commentators – even recent ones. The fate of *The Great Gatsby* is the opposite: for several decades now it has been endlessly discussed and scrutinized and celebrated. Its own exquisite economy has hardly been matched by the explosion of words concerning it. Adding to them, one is encouraged only by Fitzgerald's own sense that his early readers had not understood the novel, and that even enthusiastic reviewers had not 'had the slightest idea what the book was about.'

If it is indeed Nick Carraway's job as narrator to make the reader share his own vision of Gatsby, then that task is itself a complex one. Carraway's reactions to Gatsby are ambivalent, even contradictory. Right at the beginning of the novel, looking back on the events he is about to describe, Nick expresses a profound sense of distaste for the absence of moral discipline or decency which the story he is telling will reveal. 'When I came back from the East last autumn,' he says, 'I felt that I wanted the world to be in uniform and at a sort of moral attention forever . . .' Only Gatsby himself is exempt from this reaction, and yet Gatsby 'represented everything for which I have an unaffected scorn.' Gatsby is exempt because he possessed qualities the others lacked: 'If personality is an unbroken series of successful gestures, then there was something gorgeous about him, some heightened sensitivity to the promises of life . . .' Gatsby had 'an extraordinary gift for hope, a romantic readiness such as I have never found in any other person . . .' Gatsby, he insists, 'turned out all right at the end.' (p. 8) Towards the conclusion of the novel, Carraway is again able to detach Gatsby from his surroundings and the society in which he moves: 'They're a rotten crowd,' he says, 'You're worth the whole damn bunch put together.' (p. 160) And he goes on to tell us that he was glad he had said that: 'It was the only compliment I ever gave him, because I disapproved of him from beginning to end.' Nick's unaffected scorn and disapproval of Gatsby presumably are based on the more public aspects of his colourful life: the ostentatious vulgarity of the conspicuous consumption in which he indulges. His mansion, his car, his clothes, his parties – everything about Gatsby is tasteless, extravagant, meretricious. He seems to exist only in material terms. But there are other, more egregious reasons for disapproving of Gatsby. The novel never reveals the precise sources of his vast wealth, but the hints provided invariably link his money to a 1920s world of corruption and illegality. Gatsby is the shadowy inhabitant of a shady world. Particularly for readers accustomed to associate the heroic with moral integrity this makes Nick Carraway's task doubly difficult. How can the reader be persuaded to admire so disreputable a hero? What possible kind of greatness can such a character achieve? Reference has already been made to Fitzgerald's letter in which he suggests that there is no emphasis 'even ironically' on Gatsby's 'greatness or lack of it.' But perhaps Fitzgerald, through Carraway, does allow Gatsby a kind of greatness – the kind suggested by the positive tributes which Carraway pays to Gatsby at the novel's opening and close. Gatsby's 'greatness' is entirely a question of vision, of hope, of dream, of gesture, of the kind of imagination that transmutes or transcends reality.

Like the young Randolph Miller in the story 'Absolution' – which Fitzgerald subsequently said was a reworking of material abandoned from the opening of *The Great Gatsby* – James Gatz rejects the reality of his parents: 'his imagination had never really accepted them as his parents at all.' (p. 105) Rather the identity of Jay Gatsby springs from 'his Platonic conception of himself.' (p. 105) Like Dexter Green in 'Winter Dreams', another short story written while *Gatsby* was gestating in which Fitzgerald seems to try out some of the novel's themes, Jay Gatsby prefers his dreams and reveries to the realities which surround him because 'they were a satisfactory hint of the unreality of reality, a promise that the rock of the world was founded securely on a fairy's wing.' (p. 106) Gatsby's commitment to the world he had invented, and to his role within it, is absolute:

'to this conception he was faithful to the end.' (p. 105)

Carraway's first glimpse of Gatsby is significant. He sees him at night, standing outside his huge mansion, looking across the sea where there was nothing to be seen 'except a single green light, minute and far away, that might have been the end of a dock.' (p. 28) Equally significant is their first meeting. Invited to one of Gatsby's enormous parties, Nick at first cannot locate his host and when he does at last meet him he fails to recognize who he is. But Gatsby does not permit any embarrassment: 'He smiled understandingly – much more than understandingly.' (p. 54) Gatsby's smile – which prefigures that of Dick Diver in *Tender is the Night* – is distinctive; it contains 'a quality of eternal reassurance in it' and 'it understood you just as far as you wanted to be understood, believed in you as you would like to believe in yourself, and assured you that it had precisely the impression of you that, at your best, you hoped to convey.' (p. 54) But this sudden flash of personal charisma is in a way deceptive. Gatsby is not a social being. What is most striking about him is his isolation in the middle of his own party. The whole glittering affair seems to have nothing to do with him: '. . . no one swooned backward on Gatsby, and no French bob touched Gatsby's shoulder . . .' (pp. 56–57) When the party is finally over Gatsby is re-established as the lonely, uncommunicative figure Carraway had first seen standing in the darkness on the lawn before his mansion. As Carraway crosses back to his own house, next to the mansion, his impression is of the 'sudden emptiness' flowing from the great doors and windows, 'endowing with complete isolation the figure of the host, who stood on the porch, his hand up in a formal gesture of farewell.' (p. 62)

The sense of something mysterious and inexplicable about the protagonist is well-sustained in the early stages of *The Great Gatsby*: Carraway's first person narrative works beautifully in involving the reader in the narrator's search for the truth. When it comes – in the story of Gatsby's involvement with Daisy Buchanan – it is banal enough. But what matters is less the affair itself than Gatsby's behaviour in relation to it. Everything about Gatsby – the palatial mansion, the vast parties, the detachment and isolation – right back to his attitude that first night when Nick had seen him across the lawn, is explicable only in terms of Daisy: 'Then it had not been merely the stars to which he had aspired on that June night. He came alive to me, delivered suddenly from the womb of his purposeless splendor.' (p. 85)

When Gatsby shows Daisy round his house after their Nick-arranged reunion, the scale of the dream Gatsby has constructed around her becomes increasingly clear. To Nick it seemed that 'he revalued everything in his house according to the measure of response it drew from her well-loved eyes.' (p. 98) Nick speculates that as dreams and ideals are achieved, made real, even Gatsby must have sensed that something is being lost – the green light at the end of the dock is now no more than that: 'the colossal significance of that light had now vanished forever.' (p. 100) But this is not the primary emphasis in the reunion scene; it is the monumentalness of the dream upon which Gatsby has based his life, and his amazed bewilderment at Daisy's actual presence, that are stressed. Nick speculates once again that even for Gatsby dreams and reality must have occasionally failed to coincide: 'There must have been moments', he thinks, 'even that afternoon when Daisy tumbled short of his dreams –not through her own fault, but because of the colossal vitality of his illusion. It had gone beyond her, beyond everything.' (pp. 102–3) But this is what Nick wants to believe, rather than anything the action reveals. At this stage, for Gatsby there is nothing illusory about his 'illusion' – the Daisy he had lost five years earlier is back.

Dreams and reveries had initially translated James Gatz into Jay Gatsby. But Daisy Fay in Louisville, Kentucky, had given dreams and reveries flesh and blood. All Gatsby's yearnings and aspirations, all his half-understood searchings into the possibilities of life, had seemed to take on tangible shape in her person. She had become the ideal to which he was dedicated. Telling his story to Nick, even Gatsby recognized the implications of this: 'He knew that when he kissed this girl, and forever wed his unutterable visions to her perishable breath, his mind would never romp again like the mind of God. . . . At his lip's touch she blossomed for him like a flower and the incarnation was complete.' (p. 118) Through the 'appalling sentimentality' of this account, Nick is reminded of something, 'an elusive rhythm, a fragment of lost words' (p. 118) – but he is unable to articulate what it is. Perhaps it is to do with the universality of dreams and yearnings. We know that Gatsby's 'illusion' has gone beyond Daisy – beyond everything: perhaps it is in that 'beyond' that the true significance of Gatsby's dream lies. Not of course that Gatsby himself appreciates this; he never grasps the significance of his own yearnings – for him his dream becomes wholly identified with Daisy – thus with her it stands or falls. She it is now who persuades him of 'the unreality of reality.' (p. 106) The five years that have passed since their original encounter are as nothing. For him everything is now exactly as it was then. Nick suggests to him that 'you can't repeat the past.' 'Can't repeat the past?' he cried incredulously. 'Why of course you can!' (p. 117) Later, in the Buchanan house, Nick and Gatsby encounter

Daisy's baby daughter. 'Afterward,' says Nick, '[Gatsby] kept looking at the child with surprise. I don't think he had ever really believed in its existence before.' (p. 123) Clearly the child belongs to a reality that Gatsby cannot accept.

It is that same reality, of course, that ensures Gatsby's eventual defeat. Daisy herself is partly to blame: her morally empty, sophisticated worldliness is quite incapable of sustaining the dream that Gatsby has created around her. Her cynicism makes it impossible for her to understand what Gatsby is attempting to do. For her, Gatsby's party is simply vulgar, while Nick tells us that 'In the very casualness of Gatsby's party there were romantic possibilities totally absent from her world.' (p. 116) For Daisy such possibilities could only take the form of an 'authentically radiant young girl' who would blot out Gatsby's five years of unwavering devotion to her. Daisy in other words is firmly rooted in the reality that Gatsby seeks to transcend. In the famous shirts scene in Gatsby's bedroom, Daisy buries her head and weeps in the piles of shirts that Gatsby showers around her. She weeps 'because I've never seen such – such beautiful shirts before.' (p. 99) Perhaps in the pause here there is a moment in which Daisy understands or half-understands that the shirts are somehow something more than they seem. They are the material at the point of transcendence into what lies beyond the material. They are a gorgeous gesture, the promises of life made almost available in material terms. If so, this is the high point in the Daisy–Gatsby reunion. Daisy will soon return to the harder, harsher world she shares with her husband Tom.

Tom Buchanan is one of Fitzgerald's most brilliant creations. Tom's brutal unattractiveness – all his life has been an anticlimax since he played end for the Yale University football team – seems to keep a considerable degree of reader sympathy with Daisy. Tom's attitudes, his racism and bigotry, his insensitivity, and his behaviour, do make Daisy's cynicism understandable. Ultimately, however, Tom and Daisy are on the same side, representing a harsh reality always liable to shatter the visionary world of 'Jay Gatsby.' Near the beginning of the novel, Nick feels that he is manipulated emotionally by Daisy in such a way that he is made to recognize 'her membership in a rather distinguished secret society to which she and Tom belonged.' (p. 24) At the end of the novel, despite everything that Gatsby can do, Daisy and Tom are back together, members as it were of that same secret society. After the climactic scene in the Plaza Hotel in New York, and after the accident in which Myrtle Wilson is killed, Nick sees Tom and Daisy sitting together around their kitchen table: 'There was an unmistakable air of natural intimacy about the picture, and anybody would have said that they were conspiring together.' (p. 152) Earlier, in the Plaza Hotel scene, Gatsby had made his final effort to repeat the past – to win Daisy back, to blot out the five years of marriage to Tom, to recreate Daisy in his own image as the unwavering lover. But it cannot be done. Time and ordinary human realities come together to expose the fatuity and hopelessness of Gatsby's yearnings. Bewildered, Gatsby thinks it is Tom's accusations that are preventing Daisy joining him. He begins to defend himself:

> '. . . he began to talk excitedly to Daisy, denying everything, defending his name against accusations that had not been made. But with every word she was drawing further and further into herself, so he gave that up, and only the dead dream fought on as the afternoon slipped away, trying to touch what was no longer tangible, struggling unhappily, undespairingly, toward that lost voice across the room.'　　(p. 141)

What it is important to recognize is that Gatsby's inevitable defeat here involves the nature of reality itself. There is of course a sense in which *The Great Gatsby* is a novel of manners: it does comment on American society in the 1920s and it is critical of the corruption and moral disorder of the period. Jordan Baker's cheating at golf, just as much as the valley of ashes, in which the Wilsons' garage is situated, is an image of that corruption and disorder. And in this area there is little to choose between Gatsby and the Buchanans: if Gatsby is involved in the criminality of bootleg liquor and financial swindling, the Buchanans belong to a world which is selfish, careless, amoral and irresponsible. That it is Daisy who is driving the car that kills Myrtle Wilson is entirely appropriate: 'They were careless people, Tom and Daisy – they smashed up things and creatures and then retreated back into their money or their vast carelessness, or whatever it was that kept them together, and let other people clean up the mess they had made. . . .' (p. 186) Readings of the novel that try to discriminate between Gatsby and the Buchanans in terms of new and old money are thus misconceived. The Buchanans in no way represent some kind of old world aristocracy into which the nouveau riche Gatsby is trying to gatecrash. Tom Buchanan's present of a three hundred and fifty thousand dollar pearl necklace to Daisy on their wedding is of entirely the same order as Gatsby's palatial mansion. Tom and Daisy are quite capable of being snobbish about Gatsby and his behaviour – but that does not mean that they are members of an American aristocracy. If there is such a thing it exists, like Anson Hunter's family in 'The Rich

Boy,' only in the East – certainly not in the Middle West from which all the central characters in *The Great Gatsby* derive.

For Gatsby his wealth had always been a means to an end. But the profounder social criticisms suggested by *The Great Gatsby* do relate to Gatsby's conception of the promises of life in strictly material terms. The charm of Daisy's voice, which had tantalized Nick so long, he finally realizes is the charm of the money in it: 'That was it. I'd never understood before. It was full of money – that was the inexhaustible charm that rose and fell in it . . .' (p. 126) James Gatz's initial icon is Dan Cody, the millionaire tycoon whose glamorous yacht he encounters on Lake Superior. But when Cody is supplanted by Daisy, the aura of unlimited wealth remains. The terms on offer to Gatsby, through which he can attempt to define his aspirations, are wholly material. Thus Daisy 'gleaming like silver, safe and proud above the hot struggles of the poor' represents 'the youth and mystery that wealth imprisons and preserves.' (pp. 155–56) But that Gatsby should have come to embody his dream, his half-understood yearnings towards the possibilities of life, in such a glittering, superficial form as Daisy, is for Fitzgerald less a criticism of James Gatz than of the society of which he is a part. It is America that has come to conceive of the promises of life in solely material terms; it is American society that has converted the American Dream into the success story. Gatsby exemplifies only a process of corruption for which he is not individually responsible. His sense of the ideal is no more nor less than that which his society offers him.

If Gatsby is redeemed as an individual, it is only by the determination with which he clings to his dream, however flawed and fragile its basis may be. It is this, if anything, that makes him 'worth the whole damn bunch put together' – those who came willingly enough to his parties, but somehow found themselves unable to attend his funeral. Yet Nick surmises that in the moments before his death, recognizing that Daisy had finally abandoned him, Gatsby may have been compelled to reject his dream and look at the world on a purely reductive, naturalistic level: '. . . he must have felt that he had lost the old warm world, paid a high price for living too long with a single dream. He must have looked up at an unfamiliar sky through frightening leaves and shivered as he found what a grotesque thing a rose is and how raw the sunlight was upon the scarcely created grass.' (p. 168) In such a passage, Conrad's influence on the themes of *The Great Gatsby*, as well as its form, is perhaps apparent. What is suggested is that the existence of an ideal is essential for the redemption of reality. Reduced to its naturalistic base, reality is no more than the valley of ashes which surrounds Wilson's garage: raw and frightening and grotesque. Only the dream or ideal, however illusory, can convert or transmute reality.

It is this metaphysical notion that extends and universalizes the meaning of *The Great Gatsby*. But the novel itself, in its ending, insists on linking its meaning to the history of America. The concluding paragraphs specifically invoke the American Dream – the promise that the New World seemed to offer to the first European settlers – 'the last and greatest of all human dreams.' (p. 187) But the tone – like that of the novel as a whole – is deeply elegiac. America's history may be, as Fitzgerald believed, the history of all human aspiration; but it is also a history of failure, of dreams lost 'in that vast obscurity beyond the city, where the dark fields of the republic rolled on under the night.' (p. 188)

5

Tender is the Night

I

Published in April, 1934, *Tender is the Night*, Fitzgerald's last completed novel, appeared exactly nine years after *The Great Gatsby*. Nothing else he wrote cost him anything like as much effort, struggle, and pain. Fitzgerald's greatest gift as a writer was the graceful elegance of his prose; in *The Great Gatsby* it is the language that Fitzgerald uses that constantly enriches and transmutes the commonplace material; the novel is an apparently effortless prose-poem, an extended lyric or elegy with every word working, contributing to the perfectly shaped whole. That gift does not desert Fitzgerald in *Tender is the Night*; for the most part the prose is as fluently immaculate as ever. But the impression of an almost effortless grace is this time deeply misleading. Fitzgerald began planning his fourth novel at least as early as 1926, but from the beginning progress was slow. The mood of artistic self-confidence inspired by the critical success of *Gatsby* soon faded as the pressures of his life made it increasingly difficult for Fitzgerald to get ahead with the new novel. In 1926 he promised his agent that the text would be completed, and ready for possible serialization, in January, 1927: the first of many deadlines that he would fail to meet.

As always, part of the problem was money. Fitzgerald had to write to pay for the expensive lifestyle that he and Zelda were committed to in America or, for extended periods, in Europe. This meant that the short stories for *The Saturday Evening Post*, and the other popular magazines, had to keep being produced. But even this market, however lucrative, did not pay enough to provide Fitzgerald with any kind of proper financial security or stability. In 1924 the *Post* paid Fitzgerald

$1,750 per story; by 1929, the high point, his price had risen to the quite extraordinary level of $4,000 (the equivalent today would be somewhere in the region of £80,000). But even this was not enough; income constantly struggled to keep pace with expenditure. In 1927 Fitzgerald finally tried to solve his financial problems by turning to the richest and most glamorous of America's cultural institutions: Hollywood. But the outcome was disappointing: the script that Fitzgerald produced was turned down, and thus the $12,500 he would have received on top of the original $3,500 advance, was not paid. Fitzgerald returned to Hollywood in 1931–32, and he would return again in 1937, working at first under contract and later as a freelance, but none of these excursions into the world of films provided any kind of long-term solution to his difficulties. Yet it has to be said that there is a sense in which Hollywood treated Fitzgerald quite generously. In 1937–38, when his status as a writer had certainly declined, MGM were still prepared to pay him $1,250 per week, and it is difficult to see how he could have survived at all in the final years without Hollywood's support. But the truth is that neither in 1927, 1931, or 1937, did Fitzgerald achieve very much by going to California; as a screenwriter he gained only a single screen-credit; and his financial problems remained unsolved.

His financial worries were only part of a wider set of personal difficulties that from the mid-twenties constantly threatened Fitzgerald's career as a writer. Zelda Fitzgerald's first serious nervous breakdown occurred in Paris in April, 1930; after over a year's treatment in clinics in France and Switzerland, she and Scott returned to America. However, a second breakdown occurred in 1932 and a third in 1934. From this time on, Zelda was more or less permanently in hospital. The drain on Fitzgerald's resources – emotional, mental, and financial – that Zelda's illness produced is self-evident. Whether his own problems with alcohol were directly related to the situation over Zelda is less clear; Fitzgerald had always been a heavy drinker, and the problem would have been there even if Zelda's mental breakdown had never occurred. Certainly Fitzgerald himself came to believe he could have been a better writer had he drunk less. After *Tender is the Night* had finally appeared, he wrote to Max Perkins admitting that his drinking had got in the way of his writing:

A short story can be written on a bottle, but for a novel you need the mental speed that enables you to keep the whole pattern in your head and ruthlessly sacrifice the sideshows as Ernest did in *A Farewell to Arms*. If a mind is slowed up ever so little it lives in the individual part of a book rather than in a book as a whole; memory is dulled. I would give anything if I hadn't had to write Part III of *Tender is the Night* entirely on stimulant. If I had one more crack at it cold sober I believe it might have made a great difference.[1]

Money, Zelda, drink, the exigencies of daily living in constantly varying backgrounds in Europe and America – the complete absence of any kind of focus or order in a rootless, centreless, life – all of these things contributed to Fitzgerald's slowness in completing *Tender is the Night*. Art was increasingly something to be fitted in amid the bewildering and increasingly oppressive demands of life. At the same time, Fitzgerald's art was increasingly dependent on his life for its subject-matter. Perhaps writing about it was becoming the only way of trying to come to terms with it. The earliest drafts of the novel that became *Tender is the Night* involve a protagonist travelling in Europe with a domineering mother whom he finally murders; the pattern of development in the successive versions of the novel seems to bring it closer and closer to the experience of the Fitzgeralds' own lives.

Just how far Fitzgerald came to feel that his art and his life were inter-dependent, is demonstrated by a particularly disturbing episode in his relations with Zelda. One of the central tensions in the Fitzgerald's marriage from the very beginning had been a kind of rivalry. When Fitzgerald first wooed Zelda in Montgomery, Alabama, she was the star – the Southern beauty surrounded by suitors – while he was simply an unknown young officer. When the Fitzgerald's came to live in New York after the success of *This Side of Paradise*, the roles were reversed: Fitzgerald was everywhere the glamorous centre of attention, the successful artist, while Zelda was just his pretty wife. But Zelda always had artistic ambitions of her own. She could be a dancer, a painter – even a writer. Her decision to train as a ballet-dancer in 1927 was clearly a serious one. For the next three years she drove herself to achieve the kind of performance that would allow her to dance at the highest professional level. Her teacher in Paris felt she could succeed – even though she would never be a star performer. After her first breakdown, however, her doctors were convinced that her dancing ambitions were part of her problem and she was compelled to abandon them. Writing was another option. At first Fitzgerald encouraged her, trying to arrange the publication of the short stories she wrote. Subsequently some of Zelda's stories

[1]Andrew Turnbull, ed., *The Letters of F. Scott Fitzgerald* (Penguin Books, 1968), p. 279.

were in fact published – either under her own name, or that of both Fitzgeralds, or even under Scott's alone. The situation changed in 1932, however, when Zelda began to write a novel. *Save Me the Waltz*, which Scribners published, in October, 1932, was a thinly-disguised account of Zelda's life with her husband. Fitzgerald's anger over the book, however, had nothing to do with anything that Zelda said in it. Nor did he feel that Zelda was a serious competitor as a writer. (In fact *Save Me the Waltz* was a publishing failure.) What concerned him was that in writing a fictionalized account of their relationship, Zelda in his view was using up material that was rightfully *his*. *Tender is the Night*, still of course incomplete, would be fatally damaged if readers decided it rehearsed the same material as *Save Me the Waltz*: he insisted that Zelda agree to changes and omissions in her text before publication. The whole episode – and indeed his subsequent attempts to prevent Zelda writing – cannot be seen as very much to Fitzgerald's credit. He clearly failed to keep a reasonable sense of proportion. But the depth of anger and hostility that the business evoked in Fitzgerald does provide the clearest kind of evidence that he had come to feel that his life, including his life with Zelda, was the fundamental resource upon which *Tender is the Night* was built.

II

In 1932 Fitzgerald at last got himself together sufficiently to settle down to complete *Tender is the Night*. The general plan or sketch for the novel that he drew up makes it clear that the novel is now centrally concerned with the pattern of deterioration that he recognized both in his own and Zelda's life. Dick Diver, in terms of background, 'is a man like myself;' after his marriage, he is 'a man divided in himself.' Nicole is a 'portrait of Zelda – that is, a part of Zelda.'[2] But that last qualification makes it clear that life is not allowed to dictate to art; plot and characters draw on Fitzgerald's own experience but are arranged and adjusted to suit the novelist's purpose. Tommy Barban, for example, whom Nicole Diver eventually marries, is based on aspects of five or six men known to Fitzgerald. *Tender is the Night* is in no sense an unqualified, or literal portrayal of Fitzgerald's life.

A serialized version of the novel appeared in *Scribner's Magazine* early in 1934; the book itself was published in April of the same year. Inevitably Fitzgerald tinkered with the text between the two forms

[2]See Bruccoli, *Some Sort of Epic Grandeur*, pp. 335–38.

of publication. However, at this stage, he made no really substantial changes: a few short scenes in the serialized form were omitted from the novel, but otherwise the changes were restricted to what Fitzgerald thought were improvements in style and expression. Characteristically he wrote to Edmund Wilson urging him not to judge the book by its serial form: its book form was so much better.[3]

Tender is the Night was in the event reasonably well received both by the reviewers and the reading-public. As always, however, initial sales were below Fitzgerald's expectations. Nonetheless, the novel was tenth on the *Publishers Weekly* bestselling lists for April and May. Reviews were generally favourable, but almost in every case praise co-existed with disappointment. So many years had passed since *Gatsby*. Fitzgerald had created a situation which almost guaranteed that whatever he produced would be seen as not quite matching expectations. As one of his biographers puts it 'Fitzgerald was competing with his own reputation.'[4] In terms of the novel itself, the years that had elapsed between commencement and completion could well have had some effect: early and late material may not always perfectly cohere. Fitzgerald himself seems to have recognized this problem when he commented, 'the man who started the novel is not the man who finished it.'[5] More generally, however, just as in the case of *The Great Gatsby*, Fitzgerald seems to have felt that the reviewers – even those who praised the book – had not been particularly perceptive about his novel and its meanings. In a letter to Mencken, Fitzgerald insisted on both his degree of artistic control over the material in the book and on his purposeful single-mindedness as an artist. Apart from the opening Rosemary section, he wrote, 'everything else in the book conformed to a *definite intention. . . .*' And Conrad's preface to *The Nigger of the Narcissus* is cited once again as Fitzgerald underlined his decision to write at whatever cost as an 'artist' not a 'careerist': 'it is simply that, having once found the intensity of art, nothing else that can happen in life can ever again seem as important as the creative process.'[6]

In *Tender is the Night*, however, Fitzgerald chose not to follow Conrad's example in terms of narrative structure: no internal narrator is employed as Nick Carraway was in *The Great Gatsby*. The result is that the point of view in the later novel varies. The opening section is told mainly from the point of view of the young actress, Rosemary Hoyt, but elsewhere Dick Diver's point of view dominates,

[3]Turnbull, *Op. cit*, p. 366.
[4]Bruccoli, *Op. cit*, p. 368.
[5]Bruccoli, *Op. cit*, p. 369.
[6]Turnbull, *Op. cit*, p. 529.

though an omniscient author is also present, and occasionally the perspective shifts, particularly towards the end, away from Dick towards Nicole's perception of events. The result, as compared with *Gatsby*, is an inevitable loss of precision of focus and tightness of structure.

In the letter to Mencken quoted above, Fitzgerald seems to allow that the opening Rosemary section of the novel is problematic. As time passed he became increasingly persuaded that *Tender is the Night* would have been much more successful had he not begun with the Rosemary section but stuck to a straightforwardly chronological narrative. Some reviewers had been critical of the original version because of its non-chronological narrative scheme and, characteristically, Fitzgerald decided that they were right. In 1938, he wrote to Maxwell Perkins making various suggestions about the republication of his books, including *Tender is the Night*:

> I am especially concerned about *Tender* – that book is not dead. The *depth* of its appeal exists – I meet people constantly who have the same exclusive attachment to it as others had to *Gatsby* and *Paradise*, people who identified themselves with Dick Diver. Its great fault is that the *true* beginning – the young psychiatrist in Switzerland – is tucked away in the middle of the book. If pages 151–212 were taken from their present place and put at the start, the improvement in appeal would be enormous.[7]

In fact Fitzgerald did go ahead and rearrange the material in *Tender is the Night* in strict chronological order: such a version was found among his books after his death, with the comment 'This is the *final version* of the book as I would like it.'[8] The novel has of course been published in this revised form in various recent editions. Thus, unusually, two different versions of the same novel are readily available, and inevitably it is possible to advance critical arguments in favour of both versions. Perhaps this is an area in which readers have to be left to arrive at their own judgement.

III

In the 1932 general plan for *Tender is the Night*, Fitzgerald is quite clear about the central subject-matter of the novel: 'The novel should

---

[7]Turnbull, *Op. cit*, p. 301.
[8]Bruccoli, *Op. cit*, p. 373.

do this. Show a man who is a natural idealist, a spoiled priest, giving in for various causes to the ideas of the haute bourgeoisie, and in his rise to the top of the social world losing his idealism, his talent and turning to drink and dissipation. Background one in which the leisure class is at their truly most brilliant and glamorous. . . .'[9] The decline and fall of Dick Diver is then what *Tender is the Night* is about. A later sketch underlines the point: *The Drunkard's Holiday* (Fitzgerald's less than inspired first title) 'will be a novel of our time showing the break-up of a fine personality.' And interestingly Fitzgerald goes on to make a specific comparison between Dick Diver and Anthony Patch in *The Beautiful and Damned*: 'Unlike *The Beautiful and Damned* the breakup will be caused not by flabbiness but really tragic forces such as the inner conflicts of the idealist and the compromises forced upon him by circumstances.'[10]

Critical debate over *Tender is the Night* has always centred on the question of how far Fitzgerald succeeds in accounting for Dick Diver's decline. Is his crack-up the result of 'really tragic forces' or, just as in the case of Anthony Patch in the earlier novel, is Fitzgerald finally unable to present a convincing account of the reasons for his collapse? The problem is perhaps less the absence of explanations than the successful fusing together into a convincing picture of a variety of explanations. Dick Diver is a brilliant young American psychiatrist who chooses to marry Nicole Warren, one of his patients, an extremely wealthy young woman. From the beginning Dick is aware of the danger of becoming dependent on his wife's money, and struggles to maintain some degree of financial independence. Yet he enjoys the glamorous lifestyle that the Warren money makes all too easily possible. So is it Nicole's wealth that destroys him? Near the end of the novel he recognizes that from the point of view of the Warren family, he has never been anything more than a hired doctor looking after Nicole. Thus, ironically, her final rejection of him and the breakup of their marriage, is proof that he has succeeded in curing her. Is it the case, then, that the strain created by Nicole's neurosis is what wears Dick down? Or is it his willingness to take on, not only Nicole's illness, but the problems and difficulties of almost all his friends; is it his 'fatal pleasingness,' his willingness to be used by others, which finally exhausts his personal resources? Or is it in the end simply the self-indulgent way of life of the American leisure class – Dick's drinking and dissipation, and the affair with Rosemary, the young film

[9]Bruccoli, *Op. cit*, p. 335.
[10]Bruccoli, *Op. cit*, p. 337.

actress? The point is that none of these explanations seems adequate in itself to account for Dick's collapse, although equally none of them seems to be irrelevant. But perhaps at this stage it is worth recalling that in his sketch for *The Drunkard's Holiday* Fitzgerald spoke of his protagonist's breakup being specifically caused by 'the inner conflicts of the idealist' as much as by 'the compromises forced upon him by circumstances.' The case I wish to make is that it is indeed 'inner conflicts' – arising from a conflict of roles – that ultimately explain Dick Diver's disintegration as a person.

While the decline and fall of its protagonist is the central, unifying focus of *Tender is the Night*, Fitzgerald clearly intends the novel to be about much more than the particular fate of a single character. There is a sense in which *Tender is the Night* is a novel of manners, analysing the mores and behaviour of expatriate Americans in Europe in the period 1917–1930. Compared with *The Great Gatsby*, the social dimension of the novel is evoked in much richer detail, even if the focus remains on a selection of key episodes, or scenes, or moments. *Tender is the Night* is not a work of simple social realism, yet Fitzgerald wants here, just as much as in the case of *Gatsby*, to relate his account of individual lives to wider social and historical themes. That Fitzgerald himself identified *Tender is the Night* as a philosophical or psychological novel – rather than a dramatic one like *Gatsby* – merely underlines the point.

In this context, Dick Diver becomes to some degree a representative figure, a particular kind of American in a novel which is at its subtlest in its delicate portrayal of a range of Americans either foregrounded or backgrounded. Like Fitzgerald himself (and this is only one of a variety of points of contact between the two), Dick Diver is the rather uneasy inhabitant of two contradictory worlds. As has already been suggested, Fitzgerald drew on different sides of his own nature in creating Nick Carraway and Jay Gatsby; in *Tender is the Night*, in the character of Dick Diver, the two sides are reintegrated into the one person. What this means is that Dick simultaneously enjoys and disapproves of the extravagant way of life to which he is, with Nicole, committed. Dick is very much part of the smart, sophisticated, postwar world of 1920s America; in France and Italy he and his circle of friends embody a new kind of American know-how and nervous, brittle glamour. Yet there is a side of Dick that yearns for the traditional, more stable values of an older, pre-war, America. Fitzgerald tells us that he had been brought up believing in certain illusions: 'the illusions of eternal strength and health, and of the essential goodness of people; illusions of a nation, the lies of generations of frontier mothers who had to croon falsely

that there were no wolves outside the cabin door.'[11] Diver himself
is unwilling to be as dismissive as this. When he and Nicole and
Rosemary see the group of American mothers and wives whose sons
and husbands have been killed in the war, in their hotel restaurant,
he is impressed and moved. The group represents 'all the maturity
of an older America;' Dick seems to sit again on his father's knee
'riding with Mosby while the old loyalties and devotions fought on
around him.' (p. 113) For Dick, both the American Civil War – as
here – and the First World War are reminders of a world in which the
traditional values, to which he remains half-committed, retained their
meaning. Earlier Dick had taken Nicole, Rosemary, and Abe North
to see the First World War trenches near Amiens. In a remarkable
account of the immensely bloody battles that had taken place there, he
ends by insisting on the ironic finality of these events: they represented
the end of the old world. 'All my beautiful lovely safe world blew
itself up here with a great gust of high explosive love.' (p. 68) But
even more specifically for Dick, it is his father who embodies that
lost, older world. His father, he believes, 'had been sure of what
he was;' he had been brought up to believe 'that nothing could be
superior to "good instincts", honor, courtesy, and courage.' (p. 223)
When his father dies, Dick is profoundly affected; he recognizes a kind
of symbolism in the event, the final loss of contact with that older,
safer, more honourable world. 'Good-by, my father – good-by, all my
fathers,' (p. 224) he murmurs at the graveside. Dick is left to struggle
with the problems of his own life, his own society, without anything
comparable to the past system of values and beliefs. Clearly Fitzgerald
intends the reader to feel that Dick's slow decline is not unrelated to
wider patterns of social and historical change.

Yet at the same time there can be no doubt that Fitzgerald came
increasingly to recognize that he himself was caught up in such
patterns of historical change. Dick Diver's sense of belonging to two
different worlds is also Fitzgerald's. *Tender is the Night*, that is, like
the rest of Fitzgerald's fiction, allows its wider social meanings to arise
from a careful focus on the individual life, and in the end the individual
life in question is Fitzgerald's own. Halfway through the novel, we are
told that Dick Diver temporarily loses his essential capacity to see
and fully understand what is going on around him: he is deprived
'of the long ground-swell of imagination that he counted on for his
judgments.' (p. 98) The phrase is a crucial one; it points to the source

[11]F. Scott Fitzgerald, *Tender is the Night* (Penguin Books, 1985), p. 132. All subsequent
references are to this edition.

of Fitzgerald's own perceptive responsiveness to the fullness of life and experience – both as a man and a writer. And it is all that Fitzgerald has to replace the values of an earlier age. The understanding that the ground-swell of imagination brings, determines action – certainly it determines the actions of Dick Diver.

Dick's loss of his capacity to judge accurately is explained by his unhappiness; his emotional involvement with Rosemary and Nicole blocks his ability to see clearly. The problem is an immensely significant one. For much of *Tender is the Night*, Dick uses his brilliance and charm, his 'power of arousing a fascinated and uncritical love,' his capacity to win everyone 'with an exquisite consideration and a politeness that moved so fast and intuitively that it could be examined only in its effect,' (pp. 36–37) wholly for the benefit of others. Situations are created through which he can demonstrate his power to provide for the others: Dick is constantly sorting out problems, smoothing over difficulties. Wholly typical is the scene in the Saint-Lazare station in Paris when the alcoholic Abe North is being impossibly difficult with Nicole, Rosemary, and his wife Mary.

> Dick Diver came and brought with him a fine glowing surface on which the three women sprang like monkeys with cries of relief, perching on his shoulders, on the beautiful crown of his hat or the gold head of his cane.   (p. 94)

Throughout the scene Dick is allowed the status of an almost mythic healer, and it is in this kind of light that the decision to marry Nicole, despite – or because of – her neurosis is best understood. What then goes wrong? Clearly, as has already been indicated, there is no single factor; different elements in Dick's temperament and his situation combine to create the pressure under which he buckles (just as he buckles in the aquaplane incident when he is trying to impress Rosemary). But it is the very qualities that mark him out, give him distinction, which ironically and tragically, seem to be the primary cause of his decline. When he was a young doctor in Zurich, we are told, Dick 'used to think that he wanted to be good, he wanted to be kind, he wanted to be brave and wise, but it was all pretty difficult. He wanted to be loved, too, if he could fit it in.' (p. 149) Near the end of the novel, Dick acknowledges that nothing has changed. Called upon once again to sort out someone else's problems he knows that he will respond: 'the old fatal pleasingness, the old forceful charm, swept back with its cry of "Use me!" ' (p. 324) This, he recognizes, is the basic impulse that had made him marry Nicole: '. . . back in Dohmler's clinic on the Zürichsee, realizing this power, he had made his choice, chosen Ophelia, chosen the sweet poison and drunk it. Wanting above all to be brave and kind, he had wanted, even more than that, to be loved.' (p. 325) Fitzgerald seems to be saying that it is the desire to be loved that underlies Dick's willingness constantly to give of himself, to allow himself to be used. At the end of the novel he finds himself as a result used up – and no longer loved. That is perhaps as far as Fitzgerald himself could go in consciously understanding the causes of Dick Diver's crack-up. But perhaps the text allows us to understand rather more. Dick's 'fatal pleasingness' is liable always to push him towards emotional engagement, total involvement with others – and thus to a blurring of his capacity for objective judgement. The need to be loved is in the end incompatible with detachment, the ability to stand back and observe. Dick's outstanding qualities as a man come increasingly into conflict with what is required of him as scientist and doctor. The contradictions between the two roles destroy him.

IV

The quarrel with Zelda over *Save Me the Waltz* demonstrated the extent to which, by the 1930s, Fitzgerald had come to feel that his own life provided him with the fundamental material for his fiction. As I have said, *Tender is the Night* is a long way from being a direct transcription of Fitzgerald's life, but his own experience undoubtedly provides the novel with its main themes – as well as the source for many of its characters and events. Thus the relationship between the portrayal of Dick Diver, and Fitzgerald's own sense of the problems and failures in his life, is inevitably close. This is why what Fitzgerald did choose to write directly about his sense of personal failure is far from irrelevant to the account of Dick Diver in *Tender is the Night*. The opportunity to write about himself came not much more than a year after the publication of *Tender is the Night*. Late in 1935, short of money as ever, Fitzgerald was seeking advances from the magazine *Esquire*. The editor Arnold Gingrich asked for material of some kind and Fitzgerald responded with three autobiographical essays that have come to be known collectively as 'The Crack-Up.' In these articles Fitzgerald tries to account for the kind of disintegration that he feels has overtaken his life. When he was a young man, he wrote, life was something to be dominated – through intelligence and effort. Life was full of contradictions – but these could be accepted in such a way that you went on living and functioning. Having cracked up though, this was no longer possible. His current sense of anomie reminds him of two episodes in his past: his failure to achieve at Princeton what he had aimed at – and his initial failure as a penniless suitor of Zelda. But on both of these occasions there were compensating benefits. This time he feels only a loss of confidence in everything he once believed – 'a deflation of all my values'.[12] Even his personal identity has disappeared – 'there was not an "I" any more.' (p. 50) But it is in the third and final of these autobiographical essays that Fitzgerald arrives at conclusions that can be seen as illuminating if not the text, then certainly the subtext, of *Tender is the Night*. He had sought total isolation for one reason only:

> I only wanted absolute quiet to think out why I had developed a sad attitude toward sadness, a melancholy attitude toward melancholy and a tragic attitude toward tragedy – *why I had become identified with the objects of my horror or compassion.*
> (pp. 51–52)

He recognizes that 'identification such as this spells the death of accomplishment.' What was needed for survival was 'some sort of clean break.' Fitzgerald decides he would 'continue to be a writer' because that was his 'only way of life', but he 'would cease any attempts to be a person – to be kind, just or generous.' (p. 53) In a series of self-deprecating ironies, the tone of the article becomes increasingly bitter: Fitzgerald sees himself acting out his new ungenerous role with a profound sense of self-distaste. But the conclusion is a reiteration of the principle that the death of the man means the survival of the writer:

> I have now at last become a writer only. The man I had persistently tried to be became such a burden that I have 'cut him loose' with as little compunction as a Negro lady cuts loose a rival on a Saturday night.
> (p. 55)

Many of Fitzgerald's friends, like Hemingway, were appalled by the 'Crack-Up' articles. They were dismissed as whining self-indulgence; and the confessional mode, it was felt, giving so much away, could do nothing but harm to Fitzgerald's reputation as a writer. John Dos

---

[12]F. Scott Fitzgerald, *The Crack-Up with other Pieces and Stories* (Penguin Books, 1965), p. 48. All subsequent references are to this edition.

Passos, for example, wrote to Fitzgerald:

> I've been wanting to see you, naturally, to argue about your *Esquire* articles – Christ, man, how do you find time in the middle of the general conflagration to worry about all that stuff? . . . After all not many people write as well as you do. Here you've gone and spent forty years in perfecting an elegant and complicated piece of machinery (tool I was going to say) and the next forty years is the time to use it – or as long as the murderous forces of history will let you. . . . We're living in one of the damnedest tragic moments in history – if you want to go to pieces I think it's absolutely OK but I think you ought to write a first rate novel about it. . . .[13]

Dos Passos writes here as a highly committed, politically aware novelist, preoccupied with the impending disaster about to overtake Europe as a result of the rise of fascism and the outbreak of the Spanish Civil War. He cannot sympathize with Fitzgerald's self-preoccupation in such a time of historical crisis. In the 'Crack-Up' articles Fitzgerald had admitted that his 'political conscience had scarcely existed for ten years,' (p. 50) but the truth was that from the beginning of his career, his artistic vision had always been rooted in the individual consciousness in a way that excluded direct confrontation with social and political realities in the manner that Dos Passos suggests. What Dos Passos, however, had failed to register was that in *Tender is the Night*, Fitzgerald had already written a first rate novel about 'going to pieces.'

   In the articles Fitzgerald blames his personal failure on his inability to maintain any measure of distance or detachment between himself and the world around him. He has been overpowered by experience, swallowed up by life. He has given too generously of himself to others: in attending to their needs, their demands, he has discounted his own. Self-preservation is what he has neglected to achieve. Hence the new determination, at whatever price, to be 'a writer only.' In 'The Crack-Up' then, Fitzgerald openly acknowledges that the demands of being a man and the demands of being a writer can be in conflict. But a fearful sense that this was indeed the case had been with him from the start of his writing career.

   From Princeton days onwards, Fitzgerald had always been totally committed to the world around him: he had wanted to make his mark, to succeed, in terms of that world. It had mattered to him to be wealthy, famous, married to a beautiful girl, a social and cultural

[13]Bruccoli, *Op. cit*, p. 405.

hero. The achievement of these things meant a commitment to the surrounding world, a whole-hearted entering into it, with no holding back. Yet ever-present too was a sense that none of these things mattered very much – particularly after his initial rejection by Zelda, Fitzgerald retained a sense of life's dangerous duplicity, an awareness, as he put it in a letter much later, 'that life is essentially a cheat and its conditions are those of defeat.'[14] Such a recognition depended upon a capacity to stand back from life and observe it – even if it is still one's own life that is under observation. As an artist Fitzgerald had to develop exactly such an observational stance; he needed to be able to look at his own life, and the life going on around him, with a detached, even dispassionate eye – if, that is, he was going to be able to 'see' in a Conradian sense, and thus communicate his insight and understanding and truth to his readers. But so much that went on in his life made such detachment infinitely difficult. In the early years the pace of his life, the hectic style of living he pursued with Zelda; later the growing problems with his own drinking, and Zelda's increasing instability; the sense of rivalry between them and the consequent quarrelling; the constant financial pressures – the borrowing from his publisher, his agent, even his mother; the concern over bringing up his daughter more or less as a single parent. All of these pressures, and in particular the resulting obligations that he felt as a man of integrity he had to meet, meant that his life as an artist was constantly under threat. Writing – and in particular writing that was aimed at something else than simply paying his bills – was increasingly a luxury that he could hardly afford.

Given this overall context, the sense of total exhaustion – physical, emotional, intellectual – that Fitzgerald articulates in 'The Crack-Up' is readily understandable. And these particular circumstances are more than enough to account for the proffered solution. If Fitzgerald could only attain the icy detachment of the Joycean or Jamesian artist figure, then his problem would be solved. If his commitment to life could be replaced by a commitment to art alone, then the draining away of his personal resources could at last be stanched: locked into his art, life would be locked out. Just before sitting down to write the 'Crack-Up' articles, Fitzgerald had talked of the problem he felt he was facing in a fascinating letter to Mrs Bayard Turnbull. Mrs Turnbull had written to him of 'life being made up of hope, and a little fulfilment.' An apparently unexceptional remark. But Fitzgerald violently disagrees:

[14]Turnbull, *Op. cit*, p. 112.

The hell it is – too much fulfillment from a man's point of view, if he has been one of those who wanted to identify himself with it utterly. It's so fast, so sweeping along, that he walks stumbling and crying out, wondering sometimes where he is, or where the others are, or if they existed, or whether he's hurt anybody, but not much time to wonder, only sweeping along again . . .[15]

Clearly Fitzgerald sees himself as an example of the man who has experienced too much fulfilment, who has identified himself utterly with life, and found himself irresistibly swept along by it. Now he feels an end had to be made to such a way of living; a line has to be drawn; self-preservation and survival demand a radical change. And 'The Crack-Up', in tones of the deepest and bitterest disillusionment, defines the new Fitzgerald. However belatedly, he will become an artist only – the man he used to be, with all his commitments to other people, to the life around him, will cease to exist.

In and beneath the text of *Tender is the Night* Fitzgerald had already explored all these issues and themes in fictional terms. Dick Diver is a figure caught between the dreams of his profession and his obligations as a man. In Fitzgerald – just as in Conrad and Hemingway – work, and professional discipline, have a moral value. Before their marriage, Dick tells Nicole that he doesn't 'seem to be interested in anything except my work.' (p. 158) A little later Nicole herself reminds Dick of his commitment: 'You've taught me that work is everything and I believe you.' (p. 178) But Dick's 'need to be loved', and his 'fatal pleasingness,' combine to undermine his commitment to his work. Marrying Nicole, he breaks the cardinal rule of his profession: his feelings come between him and the performance of a professional duty. Instead of remaining the doctor-scientist, treating his 'cases', he becomes involved as a man, increasingly identified with the object of his compassion: Dick 'could not watch [Nicole's] disintegrations without participating in them'. (p. 209) The dual roles of doctor and husband are incompatible: 'the dualism in his views of her – that of the husband, that of the psychiatrist – was increasingly paralyzing his faculties.' (p. 207) Marriage to Nicole, the supreme example of Dick's commitment to those around him, fatally undermines his commitment to science and medicine. Just before spelling out the incompatibility of Dick's two roles, Fitzgerald prefigures the problematic nature of his position by doubling Nicole in the person of Dick's anonymous female patient whose body is a mass of eczema sores. Moved by 'the awful

[15]Turnbull, *Op. cit*, p. 459.

majesty of her pain,' Dick comes to love her too, 'almost sexually': 'he wanted to gather her up in his arms, as he so often had Nicole.' (p. 204) Ironically, the woman is an artist, a painter – but life has overwhelmed and destroyed her, and Dick can do nothing to prevent her dying. Perhaps echoing Zelda, she tells him: 'I'm sharing the fate of the women of my time who challenged men to battle.' (p. 203) But the major point is that once again Doctor Diver has been unable to distance himself from suffering; and what is morally admirable is professionally suspect. This is what in the end destroys Dick Diver; the contradictions in his position create pressures which he cannot sustain. As his professional status declines, he ceases to know who or what he is. He comes to realize that he has lost himself, 'he could not tell the hour when, or the day or the week, the month or the year.' (p. 220) Thus while Dick exemplifies the theory that 'the manner remains intact for some time after the morale cracks,' (p. 307) in the end even for Dick Diver the crack-up does arrive.

The subtext of *Tender is the Night* is therefore a version of what Fitzgerald says directly, autobiographically, in the 'Crack-Up' articles. Dick Diver's role as scientist is analogous to Fitzgerald's role as artist. Dick is destroyed because he allows his position as doctor-scientist to be gradually eroded. In the terms used in 'The Crack-Up', Dick has been kind, just, and generous – but rather than saving him, these characteristics have destroyed him. If he could have been a scientist only, the implication is, at least he would have survived. In *Tender is the Night*, Fitzgerald is exploring a problem that he feels his own experience urgently involves. The novel is an explanation of why it took so long to write. Being a certain kind of man has made Dick Diver a professional failure. He is allowed no second chance. Fitzgerald believes in 1935 that he can still survive by becoming a certain kind of artist.

6

The Last Tycoon

I

Fitzgerald spent much of the last year of his life working on a new novel. Based in Hollywood from July, 1937, he had worked intermittently, and largely unsuccessfully, as a studio screenwriter. In September, 1939, however, he produced a lengthy synopsis of the novel which would remain unfinished at his death in December, 1940, but which Edmund Wilson would publish as *The Last Tycoon* less than a year later in October, 1941. Fitzgerald approached the writing of his new novel in a mood rather like that which had preceded the writing of *The Great Gatsby*. He was determined once again to recover lost ground, to show what he could do, to reassert his position as a major novelist. While at work on the novel, he wrote in his Notebook: 'I want to write scenes that are frightening and inimitable. I don't want to be as intelligible to my contemporaries as Ernest who as Gertrude Stein said, is bound for the Museums. I am sure that I am far enough ahead to have some small immortality if I can keep well.'[1] To confirm his claim to 'some small immortality,' and perhaps enlarge it, was what he was aiming at in writing *The Last Tycoon*.

Gatsby had been written with the clear intention of forcing Fitzgerald's critics to recognize that he was a serious artist. Hence it was perhaps inevitable that, of all his books, it was *Gatsby* that was in the forefront of his mind when he came to compose *The Last Tycoon*. In October, 1940, he wrote to Zelda telling her his room was covered with charts describing the characters and their histories, just as it had

[1]Bruccoli, *Some Sort of Epic Grandeur*, p. 488.

been when he was working on *Tender is the Night*; however, the novel itself is 'more on the order of *Gatsby*.'[2] A week later, again to Zelda, he developed the comparison: 'I am deep in the novel, living in it, and it makes me happy. It is a *constructed* novel like *Gatsby*, with passages of poetic prose when it fits the action, but no ruminations or side-shows like *Tender*. Everything must contribute to the dramatic movement.'[3] *The Last Tycoon*, that is, in terms of Fitzgerald's earlier discrimination between the two kinds of novel he had written, was intended to fall into the 'selective', 'dramatic' category of *Gatsby* and *This Side of Paradise* rather than the 'full and comprehensive' category of *The Beautiful and Damned* and *Tender is the Night*.

Fitzgerald's remark to Zelda that the new novel made him happy reflects his confidence in the quality of what he was writing. He did not believe that the novel would necessarily be popular or successful, but he knew it was good. As early as October, 1939, when he had just begun to write, he wrote to Scottie describing the work as 'a labor of love' which is 'maybe great.'[4] Later he told Edmund Wilson that his novel was good because 'I am trying a little harder than I ever have to be exact and honest emotionally.'[5] Another comment to Zelda indicates that his confidence in the novel related to his understanding of how what he was writing represented his artistic strengths: 'It is a novel *à la Flaubert* without "ideas" but only people moved singly and in mass through what I hope are authentic moods.'[6] Flaubert of course suggests supreme stylistic precision, language used at its most aesthetically satisfying level, while the reference to the absence of 'ideas' – in the sense of detachable, abstract, philosophical themes – means only that Fitzgerald now understood that his artistic vision articulated itself always by way of the individual, responding consciousness rather than through any consistent set of abstract philosophical notions. After writing *The Beautiful and Damned* Fitzgerald, as we have seen, characteristically blamed himself for having paid too little attention to the 'general scheme' of the book: now he recognized that in his kind of fiction people and moods were more central than any kind of philosophical scheme or plan. The precise nature of the people and moods explored in *The Last Tycoon* seems also to be related to Fitzgerald's renewed confidence in the quality of what he

[2]Andrew Turnbull, ed., *The Letters of F. Scott Fitzgerald* (Penguin Books, 1968), p. 145.
[3]Turnbull, *Op. cit*, p. 146.
[4]Turnbull, *Op. cit*, p. 77.
[5]Turnbull, *Op. cit*, p. 369.
[6]Turnbull, *Op. cit*, p. 149.

was producing. And here again the example of *Gatsby* appears to have been very much in his mind. In September, 1940, he wrote to Gerald Murphy that the new novel was 'as detached from me as *Gatsby* was, in intent anyhow.'[7] It is as if he suspected that one of the reasons he had wrestled so long with the writing of *Tender is the Night* was that there was just too much of himself and Zelda in the detail of that novel. He would not repeat that mistake. The new novel would be characterized precisely by its detachment from the everyday problems of its author's life. Is it the case, then, that *The Last Tycoon* is the work of the new Fitzgerald, the new 'writer only' Fitzgerald, announced at the end of the 'Crack-Up' articles? Only to a very limited degree. The artistic stance that Fitzgerald was telling himself to adopt in the dark days of 1936 was certainly one that encouraged him towards greater objectivity in his writing. *The Last Tycoon* does, as we shall see, reflect an attempt to achieve just such a goal. But there is no way in which the novel can be read as showing at any level Fitzgerald ceasing to be a man and becoming, in the sense that the 'Crack-Up' defines the phrase, a writer only. What *The Last Tycoon* does reveal, however, is Fitzgerald's continuing awareness of the problems inherent in the roles of man and artist and the consequent tensions between the demands of art and life.

Yet if the 'writer only' Fitzgerald is not present in *The Last Tycoon*, he does emerge elsewhere in the final phase of Fitzgerald's Hollywood fiction. In the last year of his life, Fitzgerald's bread and butter writing consisted of seventeen stories for *Esquire* magazine, all concerning the same central figure, and now published in a single volume called *The Pat Hobby Stories*. Pat Hobby is a forty-nine year old increasingly out-of-work Hollywood screenwriter struggling to survive in a world where success is the only value that counts. The stories are sardonic, cynical, mordantly amusing. Pat Hobby himself, in the 1920s briefly the owner of a house with a swimming pool, is a has-been; broke, seedy, amoral, always with an eye on the main chance, but always losing out. In writing these stories, despite their superficial humour, Fitzgerald clearly draws upon a great deal of his own bitter disillusionment with Hollywood. On one level this is the dark side of Hollywood that *The Last Tycoon* largely ignores. On a deeper level, however, the Pat Hobby stories may be seen as an extended metaphor for the artistic self-definition that Fitzgerald announced at the end of the 'Crack-Up' articles. Through the character of Pat Hobby – whom Fitzgerald himself described in a letter to Arnold Gingrich, editor of

[7]Turnbull, *Op. cit*, p. 450.

Esquire, as 'a complete rat'[8] – Fitzgerald created, and simultaneously repudiated, the kind of artist figure he had insisted he would become. In the language of 'The Crack-Up', Pat Hobby has precisely ceased 'any attempts to be a person – to be kind, just or generous.' He is interested in nothing but his own survival, and is constantly scheming, usually unsuccessfully, to try to ensure it. However, there is nothing to suggest any hope for Hobby's career as a screenwriter. Such reader sympathy as he evokes is directly related to the impression that he is never going to be other than a failure. If Pat Hobby is an image of the man who has become 'the writer only,' then Fitzgerald's ultimate rejection of such a role could not be more clear.

While the Pat Hobby stories reflect Fitzgerald's rejection of the cold-blooded artist role that the 'Crack-Up' articles had ended by endorsing, *The Last Tycoon* does seem to reflect a new associated emphasis on authorial detachment. This is most evident in the narrative method that Fitzgerald chooses. Once again he goes back behind *Tender is the Night*, with its narrative looseness, to the tighter narrative structure of *The Great Gatsby*. *The Last Tycoon* is narrated by Cecilia Brady, a character in the novel whose role is quite similar to that of Nick Carraway in *The Great Gatsby*. Like Nick, Cecilia is involved in the action of the novel – which is at least in part about her – but she is not the main focus of attention. In so far as she is more than half in love with Monroe Stahr, the last tycoon himself, she is more involved, less detached, than Nick Carraway is with Gatsby, but there are advantages in this situation. If the main focus of the novel is intended to be Stahr's relationship with Katherine, the girl who seems to be the reincarnation of his dead wife, then to have the story told by a young, female character, herself deeply attracted to Stahr, nicely complicates the point of view and works against any kind of excessive sentimentality. Admittedly the text as it exists makes it clear that Fitzgerald was having some difficulty with Cecilia as narrator – but it was the kind of difficulty that the use of an internal character narrator creates for most authors. How can such a narrator be realistically allowed to know all that is needed to get the story told? The difficulty in Cecilia's case is over the scenes between Monroe Stahr and Kathleen; as it stands the text here allows her to drop out of sight, and the narrative seems to become the author's own. Fitzgerald indeed has to revert to clumsy reminders to the reader of Cecilia's role: 'This is Cecilia taking up the narrative in person' and 'This is Cecilia taking up the story.' Of course, if Fitzgerald had survived to complete the

[8]F. Scott Fitzgerald, *The Pat Hobby Stories* (Penguin Books, 1967), p. 13.

novel, there is every possibility he would have found a way round the difficulty which such phrases clearly reflect. What is not in question is that Fitzgerald had thought out Cecilia's role as character-narrator with considerable care. Telling the story five years after the event, perhaps from a sanatorium bed, her character is to mature and develop as a consequence of the story in which she is caught up. (The parallel with Nick Carraway in *Gatsby* is again apparent.) Also, by making her the daughter of a Hollywood business mogul, Fitzgerald allows her to be simultaneously an insider and an outsider in Hollywood terms, and thus ideally placed as a narrator-observer. In Fitzgerald's terms she is, 'all at once, intelligent, cynical but understanding and kindly toward the people, great or small, who are of Hollywood.' Writing to Kenneth Littauer, the editor of *Collier's Magazine* whom he hoped would accept *The Last Tycoon* for serial publication, Fitzgerald explained that by using Cecilia as a narrator he hoped 'to get the verisimilitude of a first person narrative, combined with a Godlike knowledge of all events that happen to my characters.'[9] But that combination – a difficult one to achieve – is not quite successfully present in the text at least as it survives.

Fitzgerald's plan for *The Last Tycoon* was that it should be like *Gatsby* not only in its narrative structure but in its scale. It was to be some fifty thousand words long, divided, as *Gatsby* was, into nine chapters. But the evidence suggests that in the end *The Last Tycoon* would not have paralleled the extraordinary poetic economy of *Gatsby*. The published fragment is already over forty thousand words long, and only about half of the outline plan has been covered. If one assumes that the rest of the material required similar treatment in terms of length, then *The Last Tycoon* might easily have ended up twice as long as Fitzgerald had originally projected. One may not be wholly convinced by the development of plot and action in the later stages of the novel that Fitzgerald outlined – there may be too much in the way of murder and blackmail – but that is not to say that simply by becoming longer *The Last Tycoon* was running out of control. There is no evidence of this in the published section. On the contrary, *The Last Tycoon* might easily have finally brought together the best of Fitzgerald's poetic suggestiveness, his lyricism, and mythopoetic imagination, with his detailed emotional honesty and depth of inner exploration of individual character.

[9]Bruccoli, *Some Sort of Epic Grandeur*, p. 477.

II

In writing *The Last Tycoon*, Fitzgerald, as in all his fiction, drew heavily upon his own experience. Thus he acknowledged that the figure of Monroe Stahr, the novels's protagonist, was based on Irving Thalberg, the Hollywood producer who became head of production at Universal at the age of twenty and died when he was thirty-seven. Fitzgerald greatly admired Thalberg whom he knew only slightly; the impression the producer created though, he noted, was 'very dazzling in its effect on me.' Yet Stahr is not of course simply Thalberg; Fitzgerald noted at the same time that Stahr contained 'much of myself.'[10] Similarly, there is no doubt that for the character of Kathleen Moore, with whom Stahr falls in love, Fitzgerald drew upon his own relationship with Sheilah Graham. But in this case in particular the degree of formal control, and the distancing resulting from it, that Fitzgerald achieves over the material, however personal in its origins, is such that the link with his own life is irrelevant. In *Tender is the Night* the relationship between Dick Diver and Nicole is sometimes blurred by its uneasy parallel with the lives of Scott and Zelda. In *The Last Tycoon* the relationship between Stahr and Kathleen is in comparison pure and crystalline; life is entirely subdued by art. The role of the screenwriter in Hollywood is another area of *The Last Tycoon* where Fitzgerald clearly draws upon his own – less than happy – experience. But once again the objectivity of art is much in evidence: rather than any kind of special pleading on behalf of the talented writer exploited by the Hollywood production machine, Fitzgerald seems to sympathize with Stahr's toughness towards the writers he employs. In all these cases, *The Last Tycoon* shows Fitzgerald in complete artistic control of the material out of which he was fashioning his novel.

I have already suggested that the artistic strengths of *The Last Tycoon* in no way mean that Fitzgerald has become the coldly detached kind of writer he said he would become in the conclusion to the 'Crack-Up' articles. Equally, however, his own concerns over the roles of man and writer, present throughout his writing career, are in no way absent from the text of his last novel. Indeed in *The Last Tycoon* the relationships between art and life, the artist and the man, are as problematic as ever.

The story of *The Last Tycoon* has both a public and a private face. This is something new for Fitzgerald, whose earlier novels had always focused on the private lives of their characters. The protagonists of the

[10]Bruccoli, *Op. cit*, p. 466.

two first novels choose to reject the public world: it is too corrupt or unfulfilling for them to be part of it. Gatsby has a public existence but what it is is deliberately kept shadowy and mysterious. With Dick Diver, Fitzgerald at last portrays a character with a profession; but what the novel is concerned to show is the manner in which Dick gradually abandons his profession. Thus there is not a great deal in *Tender is the Night* about Dick's actual work as a psychiatrist. With *The Last Tycoon* it is different. Monroe Stahr's work as a film producer is as central to the novel as his affair with Kathleen Moore: the protagonist's public and private roles now interact and illuminate each other. The novel is as much concerned with Stahr's role in the studio – his direct involvement in film making, the decisions he makes, the authority he wields, and the challenge that begins to be made against him – as it is with his private relationship with Kathleen.

Fitzgerald wants to persuade the reader that Stahr really is a star of Hollywood, an heroic figure, by showing him in action. He is defined by his work. He is offered for our admiration on account of his professionalism, the way in which he is on top of his job. He is efficient, decisive, purposeful, knowing what he wants to achieve, refusing to allow himself to be diverted by the scheming or silliness of those around him. In a series of convincing scenes Stahr is shown demonstrating these qualities as he gets on with his job. Yet Stahr does have something in common with earlier Fitzgerald heroes such as Gatsby and Dick Diver. Like them, Stahr is able to impose himself upon others; like them, he has a kind of personal charm and charisma that make others rely on him; like them, he sorts out other people's problems – he is the one who can salvage a reputation, stop a rumour in its tracks, re-direct a career. The difference, however, is that Stahr's kind of individual concern is used to sort out others' working lives. Once again it is as though Fitzgerald wants to accord moral authority to a kind of professionalism – as though he had gone back to Conrad, and perhaps Hemingway, in linking moral integrity to purely professional skill and judgement.

Stahr, however, is presented as much more than just a successful Hollywood film producer. He is a businessman, dealing in millions of dollars, wholly aware that Hollywood is a world of commercial materialism. But Stahr is also an artist. Fitzgerald rejects the idea that the commercialism of Hollywood means that its products have nothing to offer the world of culture and art; *The Last Tycoon* mocks the kind of writer who thinks that his art is too pure to be sullied by contact with film makers. Stahr's concern is with the quality of the films he makes; money, pure commercialism, never determines his decisions. In

Tender is the Night, Dick Diver the psychiatrist is an artist by analogy. In *The Last Tycoon* no such analogy is needed: as a maker of films, Monroe Stahr is an artist in his own right – an artist whom Fitzgerald invites us to admire for his dedication, professionalism, and personal integrity.

Yet inevitably this means that *The Last Tycoon* will continue to explore Fitzgerald's own central concerns with the problematical relationship between the artist and the man. Successful as a Hollywood film producer, what kind of a man is Stahr? With his wife dead, Stahr's life seems to revolve exclusively around his film making. He is the dedicated artist, with no life outside the studio. Is this indeed why he is so successful? When Cecilia lets Stahr know that she would be happy to marry him, he replies, 'Oh, no . . . Pictures are my girl. I haven't got much time . . . I mean any time.'[11] Later it emerges that he had not 'lost his head' even over Minna, the beautiful star he had married: only when she was dying had he been in love with her. As a young man 'emotional sprees' (p. 117) had never attracted him, and he had grown up, learning humane lessons, but never giving himself with any kind of total emotional commitment. Even at a moment of emotional climax in the novel, when it appears that by simply speaking out, declaring himself to Kathleen, he can win her, he hesitates and does not speak: 'but something else said to sleep on it as an adult, no romantic.' (p. 139) There is a sense then in which Stahr, unlike Dick Diver, is a portrait of the artist who does not allow the complexities and commitments of living to interfere with the dedicated pursuit of his art.

But of course there is no way in which 'the last tycoon' can be seen as the type of coldly dehumanized artist figure Fitzgerald had declared himself as choosing to be in the 'Crack-Up' articles. In a brilliant and haunting early scene Kathleen Moore literally floats into Stahr's life after an earthquake tremor causes a flood in the studio lot. With an extraordinary shock of recognition Stahr sees in the face of this unknown girl a reincarnation of that of his dead wife: 'An awful fear went over him, and he wanted to cry aloud. Back from the still sour room, the muffled glide of the limousine hearse, the falling concealing flowers, from out there in the dark – here now warm and glowing.' (p. 33) But characteristically Stahr does not cry aloud; and when he hears a voice that is not Minna's voice, he does not even speak. However, in the days that follow, while his public life as film

[11]F. Scott Fitzgerald, *The Last Tycoon* (Penguin Books, 1960), p. 86. All subsequent references are to this edition.

producer goes on as before, he pursues Kathleen out of the deepest kind of need. Fitzgerald handles their affair with a delicacy that is artistically perfect; the emotional honesty he aims at is triumphantly achieved, and as a result nowhere in his fiction is the movement of a personal relationship rendered more persuasively. The effect inevitably is to humanize Stahr; pictures after all are not his girl. As a film maker he continues to fight for what he believes in; but as a man he accepts his commitment to the world of experience and feeling.

Not even Monroe Stahr, however, can win. He is ill, probably dying, and his enemies in the studio are plotting against him. All Fitzgerald's outlines of the story make it clear that Stahr will die – and that his relationship with Kathleen will be used against him. Not even in *The Last Tycoon* will Fitzgerald allow art or the artist to triumph over the complexities of life and living.

III

Among Fitzgerald's many notes for *The Last Tycoon* occurs this intriguing comment on his own position as writer: 'I am the last of the novelists for a long time now.'[12] What exactly he meant is far from clear. A growing awareness of the passing of time, accompanied by a deeper sense of the movement of history itself, is manifest in Fitzgerald's artistic career. Writing now after the outbreak of the Second World War, perhaps he is acknowledging that his friend John Dos Passos had been right to remind him back in 1936 that he could only go on writing as long as 'the murderous forces of history' would allow.[13] In any event a sense of 'lastness', an elegiac feeling of the passing away of things, is strongly present in *The Last Tycoon*. (Fitzgerald had not made up his mind about the title of his last novel: *The Last Tycoon* is merely a version of a possible title which Edmund Wilson chose to adopt.) In *The Beautiful and Damned* Fitzgerald describes a visit that Anthony and Gloria pay to the home of General Robert E. Lee in Arlington, near Washington. Gloria is appalled by the way in which the mass of tourists seems to demean the house, taking away its historical meaning. The values of 1860 are disconnected from those of 1914. Similarly, in the opening sequence of *The Last Tycoon*, Cecilia and two of her fellow-passengers, their aeroplane grounded by a storm in Nashville, Tennessee, go to visit the

---

[12]Bruccoli, *Op. cit*, p. 467.
[13]See p. 72 above.

Hermitage, the home of President Andrew Jackson. Later we learn that Schwartz, the passenger whose Hollywood career has ended in failure, stays behind at the Hermitage in order to shoot himself. Fitzgerald seems once again to be consciously juxtaposing the American past, an older traditional America – the America of houses which contained 'the old American parlour that used to be closed except on Sundays' (p. 142) – against a newer, rawer, more frightening America. Monroe Stahr, under pressure from big business on the one side, organized trade unions on the other, seems to belong to that older, more heroic America. But of course the point is that Stahr cannot survive. And here once again Fitzgerald's life and art play off against each other with the deepest kind of irony. It has been the contention of this short study that Fitzgerald never managed to find a way of reconciling the demands of art and the demands of life. The best he could do was to confront the problem by writing about it, as he continues to do in *The Last Tycoon*. But the novel also continues his meditation on the meaning of American history. The passage from his notes, which was quoted in Chapter One, merits quoting once again: 'I look out at it – and I think it is the most beautiful history in the world. It is the history of me and of my people ... It is the history of all aspiration – not just the American dream but the human dream and if I came at the end of it that too is a place in the line of the pioneers.' The sense of the ending of things, so richly present here, and so reminiscent of the closing sentences of *The Great Gatsby*, is made infinitely more poignant by the fact of Fitzgerald's death before he could come to the end of *The Last Tycoon*. But what we recognize now is that Fitzgerald's art had achieved by then more than enough to ensure that the ironies of his life would not have the last word.

Conclusion

A conclusion is exactly what Scott Fitzgerald was never able to reach. Whe he died of a heart attack in December, 1940, *The Last Tycoon*, as we have seen, was unfinished. His financial problems remained unsolved. Zelda Fitzgerald's illness showed no signs of being permanently curable. In the entire twenty year span of his life as a professional writer, his career had repeatedly plunged like a roller coaster between success and failure, high spirits and despondency, self-confidence and defeatism, good times and bad. As he wrote to his daughter in 1936:

> A whole lot of people have found life a whole lot of fun. I have not found it so. But, I had a hell of a lot of fun when I was in my twenties and thirties. . . .

Security, stability, a life sustained by a sense of order, by peace of mind or tranquillity of spirit – none of these were ever enjoyed by Fitzgerald. Yet out of these most unlikely circumstances, against all the odds, he contrived to go on producing art which, if not invariably great, was certainly capable of attaining greatness. Perhaps in the end he was not wide of the mark in allowing himself, his talent, and the sacrifices it involved, 'some sort of epic grandeur.'

But it is not only Fitzgerald's life or career that reaches no satisfying or suitable conclusion. His art too remains to some degree unfinished, inconclusive – and not merely in the sense of the incomplete *Last Tycoon*. Fitzgerald's older critics regularly complained that the fates of his protagonists were inadequately accounted for – often with the implication that the author was not quite clever enough to understand the true significance of what he had managed to create. The truth may indeed be that Fitzgerald was much better at registering, rendering, and exploring experience than at explaining it. His recurrent themes are experienced in the reading, not normally worked out or resolved. Thus the sense of lost hopes and defeated aspirations, of the passage of time and the evanescence of youthfulness, of the promises and failures of love, of the meaning of America and it's unfulfilled history, of the conflict between art and life, all those topics and concerns which inhabit his fiction are made vividly present, but rarely directly analysed or commented on. Reading and re-reading the Preface to *The Nigger of the Narcissus*, Fitzgerald must have agreed with Conrad that the wisdom of one generation is not necessarily that of another, and happily concluded that the business of art is not to provide answers or solve problems.

In today's critical climate, with its preference for the open over the closed work of art, the dimension of diffidence in Fitzgerald's art is not the least of its attractions. Certainly it is one reason why Fitzgerald's fictions continue to appeal so widely and why the world he creates never seems especially remote from our own experience. Of course one acknowledges that Scott Fitzgerald is identified with a particular historical epoch – the Jazz Age America he helped to create – but it is a mistake to see him as locked into that period. In evoking it so brilliantly, he simultaneously transcends it. Here is his description of Gatsby's car:

> I'd seen it. Everybody had seen it. It was a rich cream colour, bright with nickel, swollen here and there in its monstrous length with triumphant hat-boxes and supper-boxes and tool-boxes, and terraced with a labyrinth of windshields that mirrored a dozen suns. Sitting down behind many layers of glass in a sort of green leather conservatory, we started to town.

By the end of the paragraph, the car has become another of Gatsby's gorgeous gestures. This is why we are not told the car's make: that detail would have the effect of tying the whole description into the kind of historical reality that the gorgeous gesture is constantly seeking to transcend. The gorgeous gesture that is Fitzgerald's fiction equally transcends its period. The consciousness, the voice we listen to, when reading Fitzgerald, whether naive, realistic, or disillusioned, is invariably eloquent, stylistically graceful, and able to make us feel as well as see. Above all it is a living voice. The result is an art of fiction that allows Fitzgerald at least a partial triumph over the exigencies of his life, and one that guarantees him in his own words, 'some small immortality' at least.

Select Bibliography

An important aspect of the Fitzgerald revival in the 1950s and 60s was the rapid emergence of a large body of critical and scholarly writing on Fitzgerald, his life and his works. Fitzgerald studies continued to expand greatly through the 70s and 80s with the result that the present position is that, of twentieth-century American writers, only William Faulkner, and perhaps Ernest Hemingway, have received more attention from critics and commentators. The irony of this situation would surely not be lost on a writer who, in the year of his death, described himself as a 'forgotten man.'

What follows is a guide through book-length studies of Fitzgerald. In fact the highest proportion of scholarly study of Fitzgerald is contained in articles and essays. However, much of the best of this work is contained in the various collections I cite below.

Mainly Biographical Studies

Arthur Mizener, *The Far Side of Paradise: A Biography of F. Scott Fitzgerald*, 1951. This elegant biography helped to spark the Fitzgerald revival. It includes perceptive criticism of Fitzgerald's work.

Andrew Turnbull, *Scott Fitzgerald*, 1962. A good portrait of Fitzgerald partly based on Turnbull's personal knowledge. As a young man, Turnbull had known Fitzgerald as a family friend.

Henry Dan Piper, *F. Scott Fitzgerald: A Critical Biography*, 1965. A full and reliable biography which does not really supplant Mizener.

Matthew J. Bruccoli, *Some Sort of Epic Grandeur, The Life of F. Scott*

Fitzgerald, 1981. The most comprehensive biography to date in the sense that it is an almost encyclopaedic collection of information about every aspect of Fitzgerald's life and career. Less strong on criticism and interpretation.

André Le Vot, *Scott Fitzgerald*. Published in French, 1979. English translation, 1983. Lively, European perspective on Fitzgerald's life.

Scott Donaldson, *Fool for Love: F. Scott Fitzgerald*, 1983. A psychological portrait which intelligently links the life and the work.

James R. Mellow, *Invented Lives, F. Scott and Zelda Fitzgerald*, 1985. Also links facts and fictions, but sometimes in a too colourfully speculative way.

Sheilah Graham has written three books about her life with Fitzgerald in Hollywood: *Beloved Infidel* (1958), *College of One* (1967), *The Real Scott Fitzgerald* (1976). Very subjective, with some repetition of material, but still illuminating on the closing years of Fitzgerald's life.

Ernest Hemingway's Memoir, *A Moveable Feast* (1964) contains a fascinating, if debatable, account of his friendship with Fitzgerald in the early Paris years.

Nancy Milford, *Zelda Fitzgerald*, 1970. A sympathetic account of Zelda's life with Fitzgerald.

Mainly Critical Studies

James E. Miller, *The Fictional Technique of F. Scott Fitzgerald*, 1957.

Sergio Perosa, *The Art of F. Scott Fitzgerald*, 1965. A strictly formalist approach to Fitzgerald's fiction by an Italian scholar.

Richard Lehan, *F. Scott Fitzgerald and the Craft of Fiction*, 1966. Good on such central Fitzgerald themes as the passage of time and the evanescence of youth.

Robert Sklar, *F. Scott Fitzgerald: The Last Laocoon*, 1967. A sophisticated linking of the man and the work portraying Fitzgerald as the last romantic.

Milton R. Stern, *The Golden Moment*, 1971. Again links the life and the fiction, focusing on the four completed novels only.

John A. Higgins, *F. Scott Fitzgerald: A Study of the Stories*, 1971. A useful, pioneering study of Fitzgerald's short fiction.

Brian Way, *F. Scott Fitzgerald and the Art of Social Fiction*, 1980. Argues intelligently that Fitzgerald writes as a social novelist in the tradition of Henry James and Edith Wharton.

Wheeler Winston Dixon, *The Cinematic Vision of F. Scott Fitzgerald*, 1986. A good study of Fitzgerald and Hollywood.

Gene D. Phillips, *Fiction, Film, and F. Scott Fitzgerald*, 1986. Ranges more widely than Dixon above, but less critically perceptive.

Sarah Beebe Fryer, *Fitzgerald's New Women: Harbingers of Change*, 1988. A study linking the women characters in the five novels to the changing role of women in American society.

Collections of Essays

Alfred Kazin, ed., *F. Scott Fitzgerald, The Man and His Work*, 1951.

Arthur Mizener, ed., *F. Scott Fitzgerald, A Collection of Critical Essays*, 1963.

Jackson R. Bryer, ed., *The Short Stories of F. Scott Fitzgerald: New Approaches in Criticism*, 1982.

Scott Donaldson, ed., *Critical Essays on F. Scott Fitzgerald's 'The Great Gatsby'*, 1984.

Matthew J. Bruccoli, ed., *New Essays on 'The Great Gatsby'*, 1985.

Milton R. Stern, *Critical Essays on F. Scott Fitzgerald's 'Tender is the Night'*, 1986.

A. Robert Lee, ed., *Scott Fitzgerald: The Promises of Life*, 1989.

Letters, Reviews, Bibliography

Andrew Turnbull, ed., *The Letters of F. Scott Fitzgerald*, 1963 (Penguin Books, 1968).

John Kuehl, Jackson R. Bryer, eds., *Dear Scott/Dear Max: The Fitzgerald–Perkins Correspondence*, 1971.

Matthew J. Bruccoli, ed., *As Ever, Scott Fitz – Letters between F. Scott Fitzgerald and His Literary Agent Harold Ober 1919–1940*, 1973.

Matthew J. Bruccoli and Margaret M. Duggan, eds., *Correspondence of F. Scott Fitzgerald*, 1980. Supplements Turnbull's edition.

Jackson R. Bryer, *The Critical Reputation of F. Scott Fitzgerald: A Bibliographical Study*, 1967. – Supplement One through 1981 (1984). Lists all reviews of Fitzgerald's work, as well as articles, books, and dissertations concerning him.

Jackson R. Bryer, *F. Scott Fitzgerald: The Critical Reception*, 1978. A wide selection of contemporary reviews of Fitzgerald's work.

Matthew J. Bruccoli, *F. Scott Fitzgerald, A Descriptive Bibliography*, 1972. Revised edition 1987. The standard, comprehensive listing of all of Fitzgerald's writing.

Chronological Table

1896	24 September: Francis Scott Key Fitzgerald born in St Paul, Minnesota.
1900	24 July: Zelda Sayre born in Montgomery, Alabama.
1911–13	Fitzgerald attends Newman Academy, Hackensack New Jersey.
1913–17	Fitzgerald attends Princeton University; leaves without graduating to join United States Army.
1918	July: Fitzgerald and Zelda meet in Montgomery.
1919	February: Discharged from army, Fitzgerald works for an advertising agency in New York.
1919	July–August: Fitzgerald leaves job, returns to St Paul to rewrite manuscript of his first novel.
1920	26 March: *This Side of Paradise* published.
1920	3 April: Marriage of Fitzgerald and Zelda in New York.
1920	10 September: *Flappers and Philosophers*, Fitzgerald's first collection of stories published.
1921	26 October: Birth of Fitzgerald's daughter Scottie.
1922	4 March: *The Beautiful and Damned* published.
1922	22 September: *Tales of the Jazz Age*, a second story collection, published.
1923	27 April: Publication of Fitzgerald's only play, *The Vegetable*. It failed on stage in November, 1923.
1924–26	Fitzgeralds live in France and Italy.
1925	10 April: *The Great Gatsby* published.
1926	26 February: *All the Sad Young Men*, a third collection of stories, published.
1927	January: Fitzgerald works in Hollywood.

1927–28   March–March: Fitzgeralds move to 'Ellerslie' near Wilmington, Delaware.

1928   April–September: Fitzgeralds in Paris. Zelda begins ballet lessons.

1928–29   September–March: Fitzgeralds back at 'Ellerslie.'

1929–31   March–September: Fitzgeralds live in France and Switzerland.

1930   April: Zelda has first breakdown in Paris.

1931–32   Fitzgeralds live in Montgomery, Alabama. Fitzgerald works briefly in Hollywood.

1932   February: Zelda suffers second breakdown.

1932   7 October: Publication of Zelda's novel, *Save Me the Waltz*.

1934   January: Zelda's third breakdown.

1934   12 April: *Tender is the Night* published.

1935   20 March: *Taps at Reveille*, a fourth collection of stories, published.

1935   November: Fitzgerald begins writing the autobiographical 'Crack-Up' articles published in *Esquire*, February–April 1936.

1937   July: Fitzgerald returns to Hollywood for third time. Meets Sheilah Graham.

1939   October: Fitzgerald begins work on *The Last Tycoon*.

1940   21 December: Fitzgerald dies of heart attack.

1941   27 October: *The Last Tycoon* published.

1948   10 March: Zelda Fitzgerald dies in fire at Highland Hospital, Asheville, North Carolina.

Index

Absolution, 53
Adams, James Truslow, 4, 5
Alcoholism, 38, 61, 62, 69, 73
America, myth of, 6; power of, 3
American Dream, 1–13, 59; as success story, 5; heart of, 7; popularity of, 3;
American Revolution, 6
Art, 42, 43, 82; as life, viii, 27, 28, 45, 62, 78, 84; communicating truth, 45
Artist and man, 83

Babylon Revisited, 15
Beautiful and Damned, The, 30–43, 44, 77, 84; autobiographical aspects, 35, 40, 41; flaws in, 18; immaturity of, 18, 19; links with *Tender is the Night*, 36; moral ambiguities, 20, 21, 22; narrative structure, 48; neglect of, 19, 52; reception of, 35; reputation, 15, 16, 17, 32, 43; sales, 43, 47; social comment, 39; strength of, 17; structure of, 33; sureness of touch, 33
Bishop, John Peale, 16, 18, 19, 43
Bruccoli, Matthew J., 2
Bryer, Jackson R., 30

Cabell, James Branch, 47
Canby, Henry Seidel, 43

Character-narrator figure, 48, 50, 51, 52, 54, 80
Collier's Magazine, 80
Conrad, Joseph, 50, 58, 73, 74; *Nigger of the Narcissus*, 44, 46, 64, 87
Cowley, Malcolm, 3
Crack-up, 21, 70 et seq., 78, 79, 81, 83
Crevecoeur, Hector St John de, 6
Critical opinions, 17–19

Dos Passos, John, 2, 32, 71, 84
Dreams and reveries, 55, 56, 58
Dreiser, Theodore, 36
Sister Carrie, 38
Drunkard's Holiday, 66, 67 See also *Tender is the Night*

Early Success, 39
Eliot, T.S., 48
Esquire, 70, 78, 79

Failure, 2, 8, 14
Fascism, 72
Faulkner, William, viii, 32
Film scripts, 15, 61
Financial problems, 47, 62, 70, 86
Fitzgerald, F. Scott, school, 11; Princeton University, 11, 17, 18, 19, 71, 72; army career, 11, 22; meets Zelda, 12; with

advertising agency, 22; breaks off engagement, 27; marriage, 9, 10, 11, 17, 27; quarrell with Zelda, 70; in Hollywood, 61; involved with Sheilah Graham, 81; death of, 85, 86; personality, 18; revival of, 2
ARTICLES.
The Crack-up, 21, 70, *et seq.*, 78, 79, 81, 83
FILM SCRIPTS, 15, 61
NOVELS,
This Side of Paradise, 14–29
The Beautiful and Damned, 30–43
The Great Gatsby, 44–59
Tender is the Night, 60–75
The Last Tycoon, 76–85
See also under separate titles
PLAYS
The Vegetable, 15
SHORT STORIES
Absolution, 53
Babylon Revisited, 15
Flappers and Philosophers, 35
May Day, 15
Pat Hobby stories, 78
The Rich Boy, 15
The Swimmers, 7
Winter Dreams, 53
Fitzgerald, Zelda, 18, 35, 60, 73, 75, 76, 77; broken engagement, 12, 27; influence of, 31; letters to, 1; marriage, 9, 10, 13, 17, 27; nervous breakdowns, 61, 62, 73, 86; writes novel, 63; opinions, 34; quarrel with, 70; relations with Scott, 62; short stories, 62; trains as ballet dancer, 62
NOVEL
Save me the waltz, 63
Flappers and Philosophers, 35
Flaubert, Gustave, 77
The Flight of the Rocket
See The Beautiful and Damned
Frederic, Harold, 36

Gingrich, Arnold, 70, 78
Graham, Sheilah, 81
Great Gatsby, The, vii, 4, 44–59, 64, 76; as novel of manners, 57; ending, 7; flaws, 48; key to

success, 48; literary status of, 16, 18; mature nature of,19; narrative form, 48 *et seq.*, 80; reputation of, 15; response to criticism, 46; reviews of, 47; revival of, 2; sales, 1, 47; social criticism in, 58; success of, 25; title of, 46

Hemingway, Ernest, viii, 32, 48, 71, 74
Hollywood, 61

Influences on Fitzgerald, 31

James, Henry, 50
Jazz Age America, 2, 8, 14, 18, 36, 38, 39, 87

Kazin, Alfred, 26
Keats, John, 21

Last Tycoon, The 2, 4, 8, 76–85; autobiographical aspects, 81; narrative structure, 80; reputation, 15; strength of, 81
Life and art, viii, 27, 28, 45, 62, 78, 84
Literary reputation, 3, 14, 15
Littauer, Kenneth, 80
Love, 42, 68, 70, 75
Lowell, Robert, 2

Marriage as metaphor, 28
Maturity and Immaturity, 18, 32
May Day, 15
Mencken, H.L., 22, 43, 47, 48, 64, 65
Millay, Edna St Vincent, 30
Miss Saigon, 5
Moral ambiguities, 20, 21, 36, 37
Morality, 53, 57, 74
Murphy, Gerald, 78

Norris, Frank, 36

O'Hara, John, 1, 2, 26

Pat Hobby stories, 78
Perkins, Maxwell, 44, 45, 47, 61
Personal relationships, 24

Plays, 15
Princeton University, 11, 17, 18, 19, 71, 72

Reality, 53, 56, 57, 58
Reputation, literary, 3, 14, 15
Rich Boy, The, 15
Roman Catholicism, 24
Romantic Egotist, The
Romanticism, 11, 50
Roulston, Robert, 36

Saturday Evening Post, The, 13, 60
Save me the waltz, 63, 70
Sayre, Zelda *See Fitzgerald, Zelda*
Scottie, 10, 77
Scribner's Magazine, 63
Self-awareness, 8
Self-confidence, 46, 60, 77
Self-knowledge, vii
Short stories, 13, 34, 41, 47, 60 *See also specific titles*
Side of Paradise, This, 14–29; flaws in, 20; form and structure, 24; immaturity of, 19; moral ambiguities, 20, 21, 22; narrative structure, 48; neglect of, 19, 52; personal criticism of, 26; publication of, 1, 13, 22, 23; rewritten, 22, sales of, 43, 47; status of, 16, 32; strength of, 25; success of, 23, 25; Wilson's opinion of, 31
Smart Set, The, 13, 22
Social criticism, 57, 58

Socialism, 28
Social values , 12
Spanish Civil War, 72
Stein, Gertrude, 18, 26, 47, 76
Steinbeck, John, 2
Swimmers, The, 7

Tender is the Night, vii, 16, 54, 60–75; as novel of manners, 67; autobiographical aspects, 63, 68, 70, 71, 78, 81; central subject matter, 65, 67; flaws in, 15; immaturity of, 18; links with *The Beautiful and Damned*, 36; narrative structure, 64, 79; publication of, 2, 63, 64; success of, 64

Thalberg, Irving, 81
Troy, William, 14
Turnbull, Mrs Bayard, 73

Vegetable, The, 15
Violence, 39, 42

Wilde, Oscar, 8
Wilson, Edmund, 18, 19, 32, 43, 47, 64, 77, 84; article on Fitzgerald, 30–2, 36, 39; publishes *The Last Tycoon*, 76
Winter Dreams, 53
Wharton, Edith, 47
Work, redemptive power of, 10
Writer and man conflict, 72, 78, 83